Stalin

From Grey Blur to (

Jonathan Davis

**Advanced
Topic*Master***

Series editors
**Nicolas Kinloch
Seán Lang**

Acknowledgements

The author's thanks are due to the series editors for their comments, patience and guidance. Any errors are entirely my responsibilty. Thanks are also due to Anglia Ruskin University for the sabbatical which allowed me to finish most of this book and to Rohan McWilliam for reading and advising on the closing sections. And finally to Sharon and Nina for their constant love and support.

Philip Allan Updates, an imprint of Hodder Education, part of Hachette Livre UK, Market Place, Deddington, Oxfordshire OX15 0SE

Orders

Bookpoint Ltd, 130 Milton Park, Abingdon, Oxfordshire OX14 4SB
tel: 01235 827720
fax: 01235 400454
e-mail: uk.orders@bookpoint.co.uk
Lines are open 9.00 a.m.–5.00 p.m., Monday to Saturday, with a 24-hour message answering service. You can also order through the Philip Allan Updates website: www.philipallan.co.uk

© Philip Allan Updates 2008

ISBN 978-1-84489-645-5

Impression number   5   4   3   2   1

Year   2012   2011   2010   2009   2008

Cover photograph reproduced by permission of TopFoto

Printed in Spain

P01276

Contents

Introduction

As General Secretary of the Communist Party Stalin was leader of the Soviet Union, the largest country on earth. He was the man who modernised 'backward' Russia, leaving behind him a country that had begun the century reliant on the plough and had become an atomic superpower. He was the West's arch-enemy during the Cold War and the inspiration for 'Big Brother' in George Orwell's *Nineteen Eighty-Four*. He was a vicious tyrant who had his old comrades and political enemies murdered. None of these descriptions is in doubt, but there was more than this to Iosif Vissarionovich Dzhugashvili, known to the world as Josef Stalin.

This book focuses on key aspects of Stalin and Stalinism before the outbreak of the Second World War. Having established who Stalin was in Chapter 1, we then turn to his rise to power in Chapter 2, asking why Stalin was victorious in the struggle to succeed Lenin. Chapter 3 looks at the economy under Stalin, discussing whether it was a model of socialism or a means by which Stalin built up a modern economy with little regard for the human cost. The focus of Chapter 4 is on Stalin as a person at the start of the 1930s: it assesses how the death of his second wife affected him. Chapter 5 may surprise those who see Stalin only as a vicious dictator: it asks whether someone who imposed his will on everyone else could really have had genuine supporters. Chapter 6 deals with the most infamous aspect of Stalin's rule, the Purges and the Great Terror. The final chapter examines Stalin's legacy: were there any positive aspects to his 24-year rule, or did he simply leave behind a terrified people who were glad to see the back of him?

Terms defined in the glossary and entries in the people section are highlighted in purple and blue respectively the first time they appear in each chapter for easy reference.

Jonathan Davis

Who was Stalin?

In 2006 the Vatican's chief exorcist announced that Stalin had been possessed by the Devil. For a more earthly understanding of who Stalin was, however, we can turn to some of the many books that have been written about him. The contents page of a recent book lists some of his various identities: 'Stalin as prime minister', 'Stalin as dictator', 'Stalin as symbol' (Davies and Harris 2005), while the title of Simon Sebag Montefiore's huge biography calls Stalin a 'Red Tsar'. Yet, as the title of this book suggests, he was also seen by some, for example the Menshevik Nikolai Sukhanov, as a 'grey blur', someone who was present during great events such as the October Revolution in 1917 but who contributed little to the big debates of the time. Leon Trotsky, one of Stalin's main political rivals inside the Bolshevik Party, claimed that Stalin was an 'outstanding mediocrity', representing little more than the new party bureaucracy. He said that Stalin was needed by the tired radicals, the bureaucrats and 'all the worms crawling out of the upturned soil of the revolution', whose language Stalin spoke. In fact, this view of Lenin and Trotsky as the theorists and Stalin as the organiser and bureaucrat was precisely the assumption that allowed Stalin to move from 'grey blur' to 'Great Terror'.

Already, then, we have a dictator, a mass murderer, a moderniser, a Cold War bogeyman and a servant of Satan. However, while students are right to see the self-styled 'man of steel' (his assumed name 'Stalin' was based on *stal'*, the Russian word for steel) as a brutal and oppressive leader, this stereotypical view should only be the starting point of our encounter with one of the most important and enigmatic figures of the twentieth century.

The traditional view of Stalin

The dominant view of Stalin among students is still the one that was formed more than 50 years ago, in the early days of the Cold War. The 'totalitarian' interpretation of the Soviet Union emerged as hostilities between East and West intensified. For the totalitarian school, the power of the state pervaded every aspect of society: in other words, the state became total. Mussolini was the first to use this term to describe a political system, and the totalitarian school of historical analysis emerged through examining fascist dictatorships. The main features of totalitarian systems included a one-party state, usually (though not always) led by a dictator; a continuous propaganda campaign to promote the state's official ideology; central control of the economy, the mass media and the armed forces; and a rule of terror through a ubiquitous secret police force, in the Soviet Union the OGPU/NKVD. This analysis became the established method of understanding fascism, and according to Christopher Read, using the term to describe the USSR as well was 'too good an opportunity for western propagandists to miss' because it 'tarred the Soviet Union with the same brush as Nazi Germany' (Read 2002, p. 10).

In the hostile environment of the Cold War, it was necessary to demonise the enemy. What better way than to portray it as identical to the defeated Nazis? The Soviet Union was also guilty of this in its portrayal of the West. The totalitarian school's version had the added advantage that the fascist system had just been defeated; the implication was that the Soviet Union would suffer a similar fate at the hands of the Western powers. During the Second World War, the West had portrayed Stalin as kindly 'Uncle Joe': pictures of the 'Big Three', Churchill, Roosevelt and Stalin, were sent around the world. But once the war was over, the dominant image in the Western media reverted to that of Stalin the dictator. 'Totalitarian' writers, however, were not especially concerned with the personality of a system's *leader*, as it was 'not considered critical to an understanding of the inner workings of totalitarianism' (Davies and Harris 2005, p. 4): it was the Soviet *system* that was dangerous, as it embodied ideas that were totally at variance with, and threatened, Western liberal democracy.

Some in the totalitarian school did focus on Stalin the person. Leon Trotsky had claimed that Stalin was the reason for the growth of the bureaucracy in the mid-1920s, calling him the 'gravedigger of the revolution'. The historian Robert Conquest and the famous Russian writer Aleksandr Solzhenitsyn both saw Stalin as the Kremlin's heartbeat, the sun around which everything else in the Communist solar system revolved. As we shall see, they laid the blame for the Great Terror firmly at Stalin's door. But could one man really have had the power to direct everything that happened in the world's largest country? Some historians began to question this assumption.

The revisionist challenge

The idea that Stalin had absolute power was challenged by revisionist historians such as J. Arch Getty, Sheila Fitzpatrick and Lynne Viola, who shifted the emphasis away from Stalin's own authority and Moscow's control ('the centre') to the political institutions in the regions ('the periphery'). These researchers were more interested in social history than in political history; their emphasis opened up studies based on the lives of ordinary Soviet citizens. Books on 'everyday Stalinism' and 'popular resistance in the Stalinist system' now sat alongside reconsiderations of the Purges. Rather than a 'top-down' approach, the revisionists assessed the impact of Stalinism on people's lives: how did they cope with the brutal policies of the Kremlin in everyday life?

Research into the scope, impact and origins of the Purges suggested that the Soviet state had less 'total' control than the totalitarians claimed. While Stalin's central position in the process was not denied, it was now asserted that his orders might have been used by party bosses in the regions for their own purposes or to settle personal scores. The Purges therefore had their own dynamic, separate from Stalin's role within them. To the horror of totalitarian writers and politicians in the West, and indeed in Russia after 1991, archival research challenged the popularly held view that 20 million victims of Stalin were either murdered or had languished in the prison camps of the infamous gulag.

The process of *perestroika* (restructuring) of the Soviet system launched by Mikhail Gorbachev in the 1980s aided this research by opening the Soviet archives, allowing a more complete and complex picture of the Soviet Union and its citizens to emerge. This did not mean that everything the world had thought it knew about the USSR suddenly became wrong, but instead of a *Nineteen Eighty-Four*-style image of the USSR as a country in which Stalin and the Communist Party controlled everything and a cowed Soviet population stuck rigidly to the rules, what emerged was an image of a system in which Stalin and the party leadership were not the only influential factors in societal or political change. It is these extra details and interpretations of Stalin that give us a much more complete picture of the man who ruled the Soviet Union between 1929 and 1953, longer than any other Soviet leader.

Stalin as a boy

Traditionally it was thought that the young Josef was born into the Dzhugashvili family on 9 December 1879, the date long celebrated in the Soviet Union as his 'official' birthday, but sources from local archives state that he was actually born on 6 December 1878. His birthplace was the small Georgian town of Gori. Despite having its own very different language, culture and traditions, Georgia was a part of the Russian empire, a huge land mass ruled by the autocratic tsar Nicholas II. So vast was this empire, the capital St Petersburg in the west was as close to New York as it was to Vladivostok in the east and, before the railway system was built at the start of the twentieth century, New York was easier to reach. Gori was thousands of miles from the capital and part of a very different culture.

Young Josef grew up with various names before he finally settled on his revolutionary identity, 'Stalin'. At first he was known by the Georgian diminutive Soso and later he called himself Koba, after a Georgian outlaw-hero similar to Robin Hood; his comrades would later often refer to him as Koba in conversation and written correspondence. The young Georgian saw himself as a defender of the weak, the poor and the exploited, which also accurately describes his own background. His parents were poor: his father Vissarion Dzhugashvili was a cobbler, a drunk who beat both the young boy and his mother; his mother Yekaterina was a domestic servant. His parents clashed over the future of their son: Vissarion assumed that Josef would follow him into the shoe business, while Yekaterina, believing that he could achieve more, saw him as an Orthodox priest. His father lost the argument — and his place in the family home — and in 1888 Josef was sent to the Gori Church School.

There is no reason to think that Soso was not a true believer in Orthodox Christianity, although this may come as a surprise when we remember that, as Stalin, he was to lead a fiercely atheistic regime which drove religious worship underground. Interestingly, in a BBC documentary Stalin's bodyguard revealed that his former charge would sometimes go down to the Kremlin's chapel to pray. During the Second World War Churchill was taken aback when, during discussions about the North African campaign, Stalin called for God's help: even he could not escape his past.

As a young boy Soso suffered from smallpox, which left him with a pock-marked face. He later damaged his left arm in an accident which left it persistently stiff. He had two toes stuck together and grew to only 5 feet 5 inches. This is all very far removed from the official pictures published in Soviet newspapers such as Pravda, in which Stalin was portrayed as the tall and powerful builder of a new socialist world. Behind the Soviet propaganda, Stalin was a human being, with human failings, which in his case included terrible cruelty and a murderous instinct.

From Soso to Stalin

Soso spent 11 years being educated by the Orthodox Church. From the Gori Church School he progressed in 1894 to the Tiflis (present-day Tbilisi) Seminary in Georgia's capital, having won a scholarship after graduating with top marks. He was to fulfil his mother's wishes and train as a priest. Josef became proficient in Russian while at school and proved a worthy student, with a great memory for biblical texts. Later, Stalin's excellent memory meant he could remember when individual comrades had disagreed with him years earlier.

The seminary gave Soso a good formal education and it was here that he also began to learn about Marxism. Like other parts of the Russian empire, Tiflis was caught up in a revolutionary movement as university students grew restless with the system. As the country industrialised, a bigger and more efficient bureaucracy was needed, which meant that more people had to go to university to become qualified to work in it. Once there, however, they became dissatisfied with the inequalities in the tsarist system; many emerged from their studies radicalised and ready to challenge it. The young Stalin was caught up in this growing revolutionary movement: he resented the oppressiveness of the Church and the imposition of the Russian language on Georgia as part of the tsarist 'Russification' campaign.

His move towards Marxism was gradual, and he was influenced along the way by other forms of radical politics, such as Georgian nationalism. He was an avid reader while in the seminary, often turning to forbidden texts by Karl Marx and Charles Darwin. These taught him about the struggle against authority. Soso's cautious conversion to Marxism was not complete until the end of his time in the seminary: between 1897 and 1898 he made contact with a Marxist study group, and a year later he was expelled from the seminary for not turning up for his exams (not for spreading Marxist ideas, as he later claimed). He left the seminary with a hatred of all authority, whether it was in the shape of the school administration or of the tsarist state. While working in the Tiflis Observatory he continued to spend time with the Marxists, and when the observatory was raided by the police in 1901, Soso chose the moment to leave his job in order to become a professional revolutionary.

The life of an underground revolutionary in the Russian empire was harsh and dangerous. There was little food or money, and constant harassment from the police, with the threat of arrest and exile. The tsarist secret police, the Okhrana, infiltrated socialist revolutionary groups, making it difficult for them to function effectively. Tsarism allowed no political opposition before 1905 (and only a very weak parliament thereafter), so political activists were forced to take radical measures. It was these conditions that helped to create the Russian Social Democratic Labour Party (RSDLP), a Marxist group that was established in Minsk in 1898.

The young Stalin gravitated towards the RSDLP and sided with Vladimir Il'ich Lenin when the new party split into Bolshevik and Menshevik factions in 1903. There was little chance of a Western-style democratic socialist party emerging in the conditions that prevailed in Russia, so Lenin argued that the revolution should be led by a party made up of professional revolutionaries who would act as a vanguard for the working class. Lenin's ideas were set out in *What is to be Done?* where he also argued that only a revolutionary party could lead the workers into socialism. Without such a party, claimed Lenin, workers could only reach a trade union consciousness, where they would fight for better wages and conditions but would not take the struggle for socialism further.

Others disagreed. Yuly Martov believed in creating a mass socialist party rather than a tightly-knit band of full-time revolutionaries. The split saw Lenin lead the Bolsheviks and Martov the Mensheviks. Both still advocated Marxism as the way to achieve change and a better life, but their differences grew over time. Russian Marxists were frustrated, as the division seemed to lessen the movement's chances of success, and many remained united in their work until a more decisive split occurred in 1912.

Although Georgia was one of Menshevism's strongholds, Josef chose Bolshevism: this may have been because he preferred Lenin's unwaveringly militant message of class war and revolution. He also agreed with Lenin's theories outlined in *What is to be Done?* and began to position himself as a devout Leninist. Cultural historians have suggested that Georgian traditions of resistance, rebellion, 'blood revenge' and a cult of violence all contributed to the young Georgian's decision to join the Bolsheviks (McDermott 2006, pp. 24–26). While much of the early life of Iosif Vissarionovich Dzhugashvili has become obscured by the criss-crossing of Soviet myths with reality, we know that it was as a Bolshevik revolutionary that 'Soso' became 'Stalin'.

He was a determined member of the RSDLP and was active in various cities of the Russian empire, such as Tiflis, the Black Sea oil port of Batumi and Baku in Azerbaijan. He organised bank raids to help finance party activities and gave speeches to workers about Marxism and the class struggle. As theorist or writer Stalin was not in the same league as Lenin, Trotsky or Bukharin, but he was able to convey the party's message in a way that workers understood. Josef moved from hiding place to hiding place, but in 1902 he was arrested, which earned him a mugshot and a police record with the local Okhrana. He was exiled to Irkutsk, in eastern Siberia.

To escape the attention of the police, many Russian activists changed their names. Lenin's real name was Vladimir Il'ich Ul'yanov, and he would often write under the pseudonym 'Nikolai Lenin' as well as Vladimir. Trotsky was born Lev Davidovich Bronstein and changed his name while in exile. In 1904 Soso took the name Koba as his revolutionary alias: this was the start of the move from Soso to Stalin. It was also in this year that he escaped from exile, returning to Tiflis to become a prominent member of the Marxist movement and to marry a young Georgian girl, Yekaterina Svanidze, 2 years later. She was the sister of a fellow Bolshevik whom Stalin had known in the seminary, and she gave him a safe place to return to when he was not away on party business. In 1907 they had a son, Yakov, but shortly after his birth Yekaterina died of tuberculosis. Koba was devastated, declaring that she had softened his stone-like heart and that his last warm feelings for people died with her. He left Yakov to be brought up by Yekaterina's family and did not see him again until 1922.

The year 1905 was when Russian politics erupted and the promise of revolution hung in the air. The St Petersburg Soviet (council) was established spontaneously by the city's workers. Led by Leon Trotsky, it demonstrated the revolutionary potential of Russia's developing working class. The young Stalin was active in the underground movement, urging workers to take revenge for the deaths of their comrades at the hands of the police and demanding that tsarism be brought to an end. Nicholas II was shaken to the point where he reluctantly ceded a limited amount of power to a new parliament (duma). The granting of a duma was enough to end Liberal support for revolutionary activity. Among Russian Marxists, however, while some accepted the opportunity to participate in duma elections and debates, others refused to be bought off by Nicholas's willingness to give up some of his power, especially as he clawed back most of his concessions over the years that followed. Nevertheless, something changed in Russia after 1905: tsarism had proved that it was strong enough to resist this challenge to its authority, but victory came at a price. The year 1905 marked the start of the revolutionary period that led to the downfall of autocratic rule in Russia 12 years later.

By 1905 Koba was an important member of the local party organisation, and he was invited to a Bolshevik conference in Finland at the end of the year. It was here that he first met Lenin, the man he admired so much and followed devotedly, but who, at this first meeting, proved something of a disappoint-ment. Lenin failed to live up to what Stalin expected from a leader. Lenin was certainly a determined revolutionary, driven solely by the desire to bring socialism to Russia and the world, but Stalin also thought that a great leader should impose himself upon his party, reminding members who was in charge. Koba was disappointed with the informal way in which Lenin conducted himself with his comrades. He had expected to see the 'mountain eagle' of the Bolshevik Party; instead he saw a normal-looking man, no different from anyone else at the conference. Lenin did not try to build an atmosphere by keeping his comrades waiting when taking the stage before a speech, and he spoke with the most ordinary of delegates. Stalin later realised that Lenin's modesty and simplicity were a strength rather than a weakness, but the way in which Lenin was deified after his death in 1924 may have gone some way towards creating the heroic Lenin that Stalin had always imagined.

Koba spent the next few years participating in various party activities, including speaking at congresses. He made his first trip outside Russia to go to the party's fourth congress in Stockholm in 1906; in 1907 he went to London and later he met Trotsky and Bukharin in Vienna. Koba and Trotsky took an almost instant dislike to one another, but Koba and Bukharin got on well. Lenin also paid more attention to the young man. Koba was not so devoted to his leader that he would not argue against him: he took a contrary position on issues such as the nationalisation of land and participating in the duma. Nevertheless, over time Koba became an important party organiser and Lenin came to rely on him. By 1912 the Bolshevik Party that would lead the Russian Revolution 5 years later was beginning to take shape and Koba had risen to Lenin's inner circle, though this had more to do with his practical and organisational skills than with his understanding of Marxist ideology. The simple way in which Koba explained the party's ideological message to workers made it easier for them to understand, but Lenin still thought Koba immature as a Marxist thinker.

Nevertheless, Lenin respected Koba for his revolutionary zeal and his willingness to participate in activities that could land him in exile again, such as organising bank raids and explaining Marxist ideas to workers' meetings. Koba was indeed sent into internal exile in 1908 and again in 1910, this time to northern Russia, where he met a young woman, Maria Kuzakova, and fathered another son, Konstantin Kuzakov. After another escape he worked his way back to St Petersburg, where he lived with a young Bolshevik, Vyacheslav Skryabin, who later changed his name to the more industrial, revolutionary-sounding Molotov (derived from the word meaning 'hammer'). Molotov was to be one of Stalin's closest comrades in later life. In 1912 Lenin made Koba a member of the Bolshevik Central Committee. This was of great importance: Koba was now officially recognised for his party work, including acting as a link with Bolshevik deputies in the duma and editing the Bolshevik newspaper *Pravda*. It is probably no coincidence that in 1913 Koba signed his first article 'Stalin', which, while derived from the word for steel, also sounds similar to Lenin.

The transformation from Soso to Stalin had entered its final phase. Lenin's relationship with him, however, was still not close. Lenin once called him his 'wonderful Georgian', but on another occasion during the war he quite forgot Stalin's name: perhaps Stalin was not always as high in Lenin's thoughts as Soviet propaganda later tried to make people believe. It was also now that he began his longest spell in exile, from February 1913, before the start of the First World War, to February 1917, the opening of the first phase of the Russian Revolution.

So far Stalin had shown little of the cruelty that would later make him so infamous. There are glimpses of his hard nature in, for example, his neglect of his wife for revolutionary business and the way in which he dealt with his son after her untimely death. There are also stories from political opponents, who saw in his tiger-like eyes a vengeful determination that made him hostile and intimidating. These may have been necessary attributes in the class struggle, but they also reflected the ruthless personality of the future General Secretary. It may be misleading to say that the Stalin of the 1920s and 1930s already existed in the preceding decades, but the oppressive conditions of tsarism certainly helped mould Koba into the powerful and cruel individual who led the Communist Party into the whirlwind of the 1930s.

The road to power

When Russia exploded into revolution in February 1917, most of the Bolshevik leaders were either abroad or in internal exile. Lenin was in Switzerland, Trotsky was in New York and Stalin was in the bleak and frozen Siberian city of Kureika, north of the Arctic Circle. Lenin and Trotsky had to watch from afar as anti-tsarist forces spontaneously rose up and brought the Romanov dynasty crashing down. Stalin, on the other hand, was freed under the amnesty given to political prisoners by the Provisional Government. He worked his way back to Petrograd, as St Petersburg was renamed to make it sound less German, reaching it on 12 March. He visited old friends, the Alliluyevs, and then made his way to the offices of *Pravda*, where he met with Molotov and Lev Kamenev to discuss what the party's plan of action should be. Kamenev and Stalin, who henceforth controlled the editorial board of *Pravda*, both thought it was best to offer conditional support to the new Provisional Government, as it seemed unlikely that the revolution would take a socialist turn any time soon. They also supported the 'dual power' situation that had emerged, which balanced the Provisional Government with the reconvened Petrograd Soviet.

When Lenin returned to Russia in April 1917, he castigated the *Pravda* board for supporting the Provisional Government. He believed that the revolution was passing from its first, bourgeois, stage to its second stage, where the workers would take power and lead the country along the socialist road. Lenin was convinced that the real power had already been placed in the workers' hands in the form of the Soviet. In his *April Theses*, he explained that to allow power to pass to a government made up of representatives of the old order would be a step backwards. This was a radical break with the way that Marxists had always assumed the revolution would proceed, with a much longer period between the bourgeois and proletarian stages.

It took weeks for Lenin to persuade the Bolsheviks to his way of thinking: even his wife, Nadezhda Krupskaya, thought her husband had gone crazy. Interestingly, the man who thought of himself as Lenin's 'loyal disciple' failed to support his leader at the crucial moment. Stalin, showing a cautiousness and independence of thought not normally associated with him, wavered and even thought in terms of some sort of cooperation with other socialist parties such as the Mensheviks. However, once he did decide to support Lenin, he worked closely with him in the months before the Bolsheviks stormed the Winter Palace in October 1917, even helping Lenin escape to Finland after the failure of the 'July Days'.

Opinions are divided over Stalin's contribution to the Bolsheviks' seizure of power. The official Soviet view had Stalin playing a leading role with Lenin alongside Trotsky. On the other hand, it has been suggested that Stalin did nothing of note during the year. The truth is probably somewhere between these two opposite views: it is unlikely that the party would not have made use of someone with Stalin's organisational skills when it was preparing to seize power, nor is it likely that Stalin could have moved from total non-involvement in events to such a powerful position within the party so soon after the Revolution. He was already a member of the Central Committee and involved in discussions about tactics; it is most likely that his role was played out behind the scenes, while the more gifted ideologists and inspirational speakers such as Trotsky and Lenin were responsible for the public dissemination of Bolshevik ideas.

Stalin's contribution to consolidating the Bolsheviks' power after October 1917 was more noticeable: he was made Commissar for Nationalities in the new government, the Council of People's Commissars (Sovnarkom). One of his first duties was to negotiate Finland's withdrawal from the Russian empire. Although the Bolshevik government supported this, and the right to national self-determination was part of its programme, Stalin's instincts went against allowing a non-socialist Finland to leave the newly Bolshevised Russia. He was also concerned that other regions would seek independence.

As Commissar for Nationalities, Stalin forced through his Georgian policy, which saw the Red Army, led by Trotsky, enter Menshevik-controlled Georgia and establish Bolshevik rule. Together with another Georgian Bolshevik, Grigory (Sergo) Ordzhonikidze, Stalin then brought Georgia back firmly under Russian control. Trotsky saw Stalin's military actions as a threat to his army command, thus creating another source of conflict between the two men. Stalin now began to surround himself with comrades he could depend upon, including Ordzhonikidze, Kliment Voroshilov and Semyon Budenny. These men later became Stalin's 'loyal lieutenants'.

It was in this period that Lenin began to see Stalin as wilful, even brutal. The Civil War had a profound effect on the Bolshevik Party, altering its nature and shaping the way it would view the world. It also contributed to the way Stalin interpreted things: he saw belligerency and coercive measures as a way to solve problems. Lenin found these traits useful as he knew that Stalin could get things done, but the Georgian affair opened Lenin's eyes: he was concerned at the oppressive way in which Stalin dealt with the nationalities question.

Amid the revolutionary turmoil and war, Stalin found time to marry again. His second wife was the young Bolshevik daughter of his old friends, the Alliluyevs. Nadezhda Alliluyeva, known as Nadya, was Stalin's secretary, and was 17 or 18 when the two married in 1918 or 1919. Theirs was a passionate marriage, filled both with love and hate, and they had two children, Vasily in 1921 and Svetlana in 1926. Stalin was happy to have young Nadya as his companion when he was appointed Political Commissar to the Southwestern Front in 1920. It was here that he fell out with another important party member, Mikhail Tukhachevsky, commanding the troops pushing west in the war with Poland. Even after 17 years had passed, Stalin never forgot crossing swords with Tukhachevsky: the military commander was murdered in the Purges in 1937. For now, though, Stalin was content with securing his position in the party. Lenin thought him an invaluable member of the Central Committee and of the Politburo, and Stalin embraced his role as one of Lenin's chief organisers. He was also a member of the Organisational Bureau (Orgburo), which controlled who held which position in the party. This meant that he had a place in three of the most important bodies in the party. However, by 1922 Lenin had begun to realise that Stalin might pose a danger both to the party and to the country.

Conclusion

The transition from the young Josef to the revolutionary Stalin was not inevitable, but there were certain factors that made it likely. The environment in which Soso grew up was violent, oppressive and revolutionary. He was an intelligent child who flourished in education, whether the formal teaching of the seminary or the informal teachings of the Marxists with whom he spent his formative years. He saw himself as a class warrior and a champion of the oppressed, as is shown by his taking the name Koba. This drew him not only to Marxism but specifically to Bolshevik Marxism, probably because of its rigid revolutionary purpose.

It was his skills as an organiser rather than his knowledge of Marxist theory that helped him make his name and ultimately won him the trust of Lenin. Yet although he grew even closer to Lenin during the latter part of the Civil War,

Lenin was wary of Stalin's growing power and the ways in which he used it. Stalin had alienated some influential people along the way: he fell out with Trotsky, with whom he struggled in the 1920s, and with Yakov Sverdlov, the Bolshevik Party's chief administrator. After Sverdlov's unexpectedly early death in 1919, the party needed someone to fill his position, although it was not one that ideologists such as Trotsky or Bukharin wanted: they viewed it as little more than organising the names of the party membership and they were happy when Stalin took the job of General Secretary. His administrative role earned Stalin the light-hearted nickname 'Comrade Card Index': underestimating the importance of Stalin's new position in the party was the Bolsheviks' first mistake.

Questions

1 The 'totalitarian' school and the revisionist school have different interpretations of Stalin's rule. With which interpretation do you think Stalin himself would have agreed?

2 Which details of Stalin's early life do you consider most significant, and why?

3 How did Stalin's personal life and character determine his role within the party?

References

- Davies, S., and Harris, J. (eds) (2005) *Stalin: A New History*, Cambridge University Press.
- McDermott, K. (2006) *Stalin: Revolutionary in an Era of War*, Palgrave Macmillan.
- Read, C. (ed.) (2003) *The Stalin Years: A Reader*, Palgrave Macmillan.

After Lenin: why Stalin?

At 6.50 p.m. on 21 January 1924, Vladimir Il'ich Lenin died in his house in Gorky. In the final months before his death he was unaware that there was a struggle going on for control of the Communist Party, as Krupskaya shielded him from all internal arguments. Officially Lenin had only been *de facto* leader of the party, so there was no established process to govern the fight to succeed him. He thought that a collective leadership should be established, partly because he did not believe that any one person in the Politburo was capable of successfully leading it alone. Stalin thought differently, and after Lenin's death he quickly set about becoming leader both of the party and of the country. He was a shrewd politician, but it is too simplistic to ascribe his rise to power purely to his personal efforts. The General Secretary certainly played the system better than the other Bolsheviks, but in the period immediately after Lenin's death Stalin was not seen as the natural heir: the logical successor seemed to be his bitter enemy Trotsky. Nevertheless, by the end of the 1920s Josef Stalin was the most powerful man in the Soviet Union. His rise to the position of first among equals is a story of intrigue, betrayal, political manoeuvrings and failure within the Communist Party, but he also enjoyed growing support from sections of society who needed to see the party deliver more of the promises it had made before and during the October Revolution. Many Russians came to see Stalin as the right person to lead Russia's oppressed masses to the promised land of communism.

Lenin's last years

As the Civil War drew to a close, the leaders of Soviet Russia were beset by new problems. The country's economy and infrastructure had been devastated by war, revolution and foreign intervention. The radical policy of war communism, whereby the state took control of large factories and forcibly requisitioned grain from the peasants, had proved unsuccessful. The Kronstadt Mutiny, a revolt by sailors at the naval garrison of Kronstadt in 1921, together with other uprisings, convinced Lenin that a new course had to be set. At the Tenth Party Congress, he declared a New Economic Policy (NEP) allowing a mixed economy of state-owned and private property. The aim was to build an alliance (*smychka*) between workers in the cities and peasants in the countryside — hence the symbol of the hammer and sickle on the Soviet Union's flag. The NEP lasted for most of the decade, and so did the debate over whether it was to be a long-term plan to reach socialism or a short-term retreat to give the Communists some breathing space. This argument over how quickly the country should move to socialism contributed greatly to the power struggle after Lenin's death.

Another important development at this congress was the banning of political factions inside the party. By this time Soviet Russia was a one-party state. A one-party state can still allow open debate and the freedom to criticise the government's actions but the curtailing of dissent within the Russian Communist Party ended these crucial rights and tightened the leader's control. Stalin supported Lenin in this move, and Lenin had grown accustomed to having Stalin firmly on his side. It is likely that this was why Lenin supported Kamenev's suggestion that Stalin be made General Secretary of the party. This job involved managing party affairs; together with all his other bureaucratic roles, it ensured that Stalin gained a firm grip on the levers of power.

Stalin's grasp on power was momentarily loosened by a falling-out with Lenin in 1922. Two issues led Lenin to reconsider Stalin's position in the party. The first grew out of the controversial way in which Stalin and Ordzhonikidze had forced Georgia back under Russian control. We have already seen how concerned Lenin was about Stalin's willingness to use oppressive measures when he was Commissar for Nationalities; this had led to serious clashes between the two men over Stalin's plans to incorporate other republics, including Georgia, Ukraine and Belarus, into the RSFSR. Stalin wanted them to be brought in as autonomous republics, but with little autonomy; Lenin saw this as the assertion of something he loathed: 'Great Russian chauvinism'. The second issue was an argument Stalin had with Lenin's wife, Krupskaya.

In 1918 Lenin survived an assassination attempt, but the bullet remained lodged in his body until his death. It is generally believed that this contributed to his poor health: he suffered three strokes between 1922 and 1923, each one leaving him weaker and more paralysed than the last. Krupskaya wanted to care for her husband but Stalin had hoped to take this responsibility himself. This can be seen either as the desire of a good friend to help his comrade return to health or as a cynical move to ensure that only Stalin had access to Lenin and could therefore control the flow of news between Lenin and the party. Stalin was wary of others discussing political matters with Lenin, so when he discovered that Lenin and Krupskaya had been talking about politics at greater length than the doctors allowed he was outraged. In a telephone conversation with Krupskaya, Stalin swore at her, calling her by an outrageous name. She did not tell Lenin about this at the time, but he found out a few months later and forced Stalin to apologise.

The row with Krupskaya and concerns over Stalin's ideas about the roles for the republics in what would soon become the Soviet Union led to Lenin's reassessment of Stalin. In his 1922 *Letter to the Congress*, better known as his 'Testament', Lenin outlined his feelings about all the leading Bolsheviks in the party. Bukharin was a 'brilliant theoretician' and the favourite of the whole party, but Lenin thought his thinking not entirely Marxist; Trotsky had 'outstanding ability' and was 'personally perhaps the most capable man' in the Central Committee, but 'displayed excessive self-assurance' and was preoccupied with the 'purely administrative side of the work'. Lenin noted that as General Secretary, Stalin had unlimited authority concentrated in his hands, and he declared himself unsure 'whether he will always be capable of using that authority with sufficient caution'. Lenin's disillusionment with Stalin was made even more noticeable in January 1923 when he added a special note, before he had even learned of Stalin's argument with Krupskaya, saying, 'Stalin is too rude and this defect…becomes intolerable in a General Secretary.' He suggested that 'the comrades think of a way of removing Stalin from that post', replacing him with someone 'more tolerant, more loyal, more polite and more considerate'. This move to replace Stalin was part of Lenin's 'last struggle' against the party's bureaucracy, which he felt had grown too powerful. He believed that a collective leadership should follow him, rather than rule by any one individual, but because he was critical about each candidate his wishes were not made public. When Lenin's private secretary showed the Testament to Stalin, he ordered her to burn it. Lenin, unaware of this, asked his secretary the next day to keep the document secret; she therefore made a copy to replace the burnt original.

Lenin was concerned that the differences within the party would lead to major problems between comrades, particularly Trotsky and Stalin. He was right, though the feud between the two men was kept hidden from him as he was too ill to be told of anything so damaging to the party. By the end of 1923 Lenin's health had deteriorated badly and on 21 January 1924 he died.

The power struggle: the opening shots

Shortly after his death, Lenin was reborn in a form more like the leader that Stalin had always thought he should be: the great 'mountain eagle' of the socialist movement. Lenin was canonised in the new Soviet 'religion' and would soon be deified in the emerging Stalinist 'church'. Stalin ignored the dead leader's wish (and Krupskaya's) that he be buried next to his mother in St Petersburg; instead Lenin was entombed in a mausoleum in Moscow's Red Square, where he is still on show for the world to see. This was the first stage in the creation of the 'Cult of Lenin', the phenomenon constructed and used by Stalin to push himself into a primary position in the post-Lenin leadership struggle. There had been nothing like a cult of personality while Lenin was alive. Posters featuring Lenin's picture were so rare that those outside the party often did not know him by sight: once he was even arrested by a group of young Communists who did not recognise him. There had been no constant quoting of speeches by the 'Great Leader' while Lenin was alive; he found the promotion of his person deeply unpleasant. When his friend Maksim Gorky referred to Lenin as a saint, he was formally reprimanded by the Politburo. Building up Lenin posthumously to be a national hero, however, gave Stalin a powerful and effective weapon with which to fight for the position of leader and enabled him to dictate the rules of the ensuing leadership campaign. In effect it came down to a competition to see who could prove himself the best Leninist.

The way that this game would be played became clear as early as Lenin's funeral. Trotsky was away from Moscow convalescing, and Stalin told him not to worry about returning for the ceremony; it is even alleged that Stalin gave him the wrong date. Trotsky's absence did not go unnoticed: other comrades saw it as a great insult to Lenin and his memory. Stalin had delivered the first blow against his arch-rival; it also put him in a strong position to make quasi-religious speeches about Lenin at the funeral and to portray himself as Lenin's main 'disciple'. He followed this up with a series of lectures, *The Foundations of Leninism*, in which he coined the term 'Leninism' (which later became known as Marxism-Leninism, the official ideology of the USSR, and even, briefly, Marxism-Leninism-Stalinism). Lenin's words became sacred: anyone who deviated from them was accused of 'factionalism', which had been outlawed in 1921. The foundations for Stalin's path to power had thus been laid. This did not mean, however, that it would lead inevitably to the top job: other comrades were also making their way there. How could Stalin ensure that he succeeded Lenin?

In some ways he did not have to. Stalin did not simply manoeuvre himself into pole position, although he certainly manipulated situations. He seized opportunities to take advantage of his opponents, either because they managed their own campaigns poorly or because they trusted him too much. He soon made them pay for that trust as, one by one, he turned against them; yet he was too clever to stage a public falling-out: he left infighting to others. Thus Stalin was able to portray himself as exactly what the party needed at any given time: he was a moderate when Trotsky was a radical and a radical when Bukharin was a moderate. This suggests that there were other forces at work apart from Stalin's manipulative arts: he was better at tapping in to the mood of the party than his rivals.

Stalin, Trotsky and the Left Opposition

The personal animosity between Stalin and Trotsky was evident in the 1920s. Stalin feared Trotsky because of his closeness to Lenin; many saw Trotsky as Lenin's natural successor. Trotsky's position as head of the Red Army led to allegations by Stalin, Grigory Zinoviev and Lev Kamenev that he would lead a coup against the party leadership and become a dictator. They claimed that Trotsky saw himself as a Bonaparte figure, an allegation he flatly denied.

Differences over policy also drove the two men into different camps. Trotsky took a different view from Stalin over the development of socialism. The question of how quickly socialism should be constructed in the USSR formed the basis of most discussions in the party in the 1920s. The Left Opposition, which included Trotsky, Karl Radek and Yevgeny Preobrazhensky, was united in its belief that socialism had to be built quickly through rapid industrialisation. This was the more ideologically sound approach, as it would create the larger proletariat which was fundamental for the successful implementation of Marxist ideals. The problem for the Bolsheviks (by now working under their new name, the Communist Party) was that the working class had always been smaller in numbers than the Russian peasantry. This situation grew worse during the Civil War, because many of the most socialist workers and loyal Communists were killed fighting for the revolutionary cause against the Whites. Many others left the towns and returned to the countryside in search of food.

The Left Opposition's plans for the construction of socialism would, in theory, help to create a larger and more loyal support base than the peasantry offered. However, according to others in the party, who came to be known as the Right Opposition, this would alienate the peasants and could lead to social unrest. The 'Rightists' were not against industrialising, but they argued that it should proceed at a slower place. Both groups claimed their ideas represented what Lenin himself would have done.

Towards the end of 1923, Trotsky wrote to the Central Committee with concerns about the growing strength of the bureaucracy inside the Communist Party, and the disastrous effect this was having on its internal democracy. He noted that members were more interested in following the Secretariat's line because it appeared that its opinions were the opinions of the party as a whole. This meant that the power in the party was shifting away from idealists who wanted to build a socialist society and towards 'careerists' who cared more about securing jobs for themselves.

A week later, a declaration from another 46 leading Bolsheviks supported Trotsky and criticised the Politburo's bureaucratic and undemocratic practices. They were also critical of economic decisions that had failed to meet the needs of the country. They called for the right to form factions, believing that this would lead to the restoration of party democracy and therefore a more vibrant and ideologically driven government. Zinoviev, Kamenev and Stalin all felt themselves under attack from people who appeared to endorse Trotsky's arguments, so they joined together in a triumvirate, or *troika*, against growing 'Trotskyism' within the Communist Party. They dismissed Trotsky's criticisms and the 'Declaration of the 46' as renewed factionalism, outlawed at the Tenth Party Congress in 1921. An anti-Trotskyist bloc had clearly emerged some months before Lenin's death, and the situation would only get worse for Trotsky. To understand why, we need to outline his ideas and policies.

It has already been noted that the Left Opposition envisaged rapid industrialisation based on socialist lines, emphasising commitment to the working class. This set them against the peasantry and threatened the *smychka* between the workers and peasants, which in turn allowed the triumvirate to portray the Leftists as anti-Leninist. They claimed that Lenin had wanted the NEP to last 'for a generation', whereas Trotsky and Preobrazhensky argued that it was only meant as a temporary measure to stabilise the Soviet economy until the time was right to move on to socialism.

Trotsky also clashed with the triumvirate over the spreading of the revolution outside Russia. Both Lenin and Trotsky were internationalists and believed that socialism could not be built in one country alone. The Left Opposition put their faith in the revolution acting as a spark that would inspire workers in industrialised countries to follow their Russian comrades' example and replace capitalism with socialism. There would then be a huge socialist federation, which would save the revolution in Russia from its pressing economic and social problems. However, the revolution did not spread to the industrialised countries of western Europe after 1917, despite attempts and false starts in Germany and Hungary and the Red Army's efforts in Poland during the Civil War. International revolution became less likely and Stalin and his clique turned this into another stick with which to beat Trotsky. Although it was a highly un-Leninist stance, the Stalinist centre adopted a more 'patriotic' position, focusing their rhetoric on the strength of the Russian workers. Stalin asked why Trotsky did not believe that Russians could build socialism on their own; did he have no faith in them? Bukharin spoke of 'Socialism in One Country', a slogan that later became synonymous with Stalinism. This smacked of the 'Great Russian chauvinism' which Lenin had so detested, but it was more appealing to Russian party members than Trotsky's internationalism. His alienation from his own party had begun.

Part of the problem for Trotsky was that he had little interest in the political intrigue and manoeuvrings that go with a power struggle. Stalin seemed to thrive on manipulating situations, whereas Trotsky believed that his ideas would win him support on their own merits. Trotsky was undoubtedly one of the great intellectuals of the party, but he was widely seen as too clever: party members often had difficulty understanding his ideas. Stalin, on the other hand, pitched his ideas at a level that everyone could understand. Perhaps Trotsky was still talking to the more ideologically aware people who had made up the party membership in the days before the Civil War, when Bolsheviks had been professional revolutionaries who understood the finer points of Marx. If so, he had failed to recognise the profound shift in the nature of the post-Civil War party membership: many new members were only semi-literate and had joined the Communists because it was the best way to ensure a better standard of living in a war-torn country. It was highly unlikely that they would be able to understand the finer details of Marxist dialectic. This is not to suggest that *all* new members who became Communists did so without any political belief, but it is important to remember that the Communist Party of the 1920s was radically different from the Bolshevik Party of the 1910s. Stalin understood this much better than Trotsky.

In 1925, Trotsky was replaced as head of the Red Army by Mikhail Frunze. Trotsky thought that this would reduce the accusations that he wanted to set up a Bonapartist dictatorship, but in fact it left him isolated in the party, as a potential powerbase had been removed. At the same time, Stalin, in his capacity as General Secretary, had Trotsky's supporters removed from key positions in the upper echelons of the Communist Party. Trotsky was now being out-manoeuvred tactically as well as ideologically.

Freed from his military role, Trotsky published *Lessons of October*, in which he criticised Zinoviev and Kamenev for lacking revolutionary fervour; he also implied that they were to blame for the growing strength of the bureaucracy. Free debate and expression of different opinions may be integral to democracy, both inside and outside a party, but Trotsky's criticisms of his comrades did nothing to endear him to them. In response, his opponents reminded the party that Trotsky had been a Menshevik for a long time before he joined the Bolsheviks and that he had had many political clashes with Lenin. Even though this had been before Trotsky became a loyal Bolshevik, and despite the fact that in some ways, including over the crucial question of permanent revolution, Lenin had actually adopted Trotsky's position, it was used to portray him as anti-Leninist, an almost blasphemous position in the new 'Age of Lenin'.

Trotsky's downfall was not complete until the late 1920s. In 1927 he was expelled from the party and in 1929 he was exiled from the Soviet Union. On 20 January 1929 he was handed a copy of minutes from a secret police meeting where 'the case of Citizen Trotsky, Lev Davidovich' was considered. It was resolved that he was 'to be deported from the territory of the USSR'. Unwillingly, Trotsky moved first to Constantinople and eventually to Mexico, where he met his ultimate fate in 1940 at the hands of a Stalinist agent. However, his fate had been sealed by the mid-1920s, when the triumvirate manoeuvred him out of the running for the position of leader. Trotsky was tactically inept and lacked the necessary skills to take on someone with the manipulative skills of Stalin, whose hold over the workings of the Communist Party prevented the Left Opposition's message from reaching a wide audience and ensured that Trotsky's supporters were removed from powerful positions. Trotsky's timing was poor: he published criticisms of his comrades when he should have been looking to them for support, even if this could have been seen as engaging in factionalism. Trotsky had no real desire to use political tactics to win the power struggle; he believed that his ideas would prove more important on their own merits. He stood little chance against a powerful opponent like Stalin, who was willing to do whatever it took to become leader.

The United Opposition

Once Trotsky had been removed as a political threat, Stalin wasted no time in turning against his allies Zinoviev and Kamenev. Both men had grown concerned at Stalin's power in the party and at his identification of himself as Lenin's closest and most loyal follower. The attacks were not simply personal: Zinoviev also criticised the pro-peasant economic policy the party had adopted. This was largely Bukharin's work. He opposed the rapid industrialisation proposed by Trotsky and the Left Opposition and thought that the NEP should be allowed time to develop: socialism could come about gradually through the alliance between workers and peasants. Zinoviev, however, argued that the kulaks (rich peasants) were holding the party to ransom. While Kamenev sided with Zinoviev, Stalin agreed with Bukharin, but he let the three of them argue among themselves, giving the impression that he was above the squabbles in the party.

Despite the fear and loathing they had professed for Trotsky when they were allied to Stalin, Zinoviev and Kamenev now joined their former foe in creating the United Opposition to Stalin in 1926 after the triumvirate broke up. However, the time for challenging Stalin with any hope of success had passed. Just as he had done with Trotsky, Stalin used his administrative position to remove both men from the Politburo, where their seats went to Stalin's supporters, and from their positions as leaders of the party in Leningrad (Zinoviev) and Moscow (Kamenev). Zinoviev was also replaced as head of the Comintern.

Stalin removed his opponents' supporters from key positions in the party and replaced them with his own supporters. This created a 'circular flow of power': people at all levels of the party owed their positions, and the promise of higher ones, to Stalin and therefore supported him in crucial votes at party congresses. This may explain why Kamenev was shouted down at the Fourteenth Party Congress in 1925 when he demanded that Stalin be removed from his position for his abuses of power; delegates showed their support for Stalin by giving him a standing ovation. With his supporters in place at all levels of the party, it was easy for Stalin to ensure that the United Opposition did not spread its ideas too widely: as a result it only lasted a year and a half, from mid-1926 to the end of 1927. By the Fifteenth Party Congress in 1927, all Oppositionists had been expelled from the party. Stalin was now in an even stronger position.

Stalin's break with the Right Opposition

With the Left and United Oppositions defeated, it appeared that Stalin and his comrades in the Right Opposition, Bukharin, Rykov and Tomsky, could now pursue a gradualist and pro-peasant policy. Much to Bukharin's surprise, however, Stalin suddenly turned against him and his ideas. Stalin declared that the time was right to resume the socialist offensive and he challenged the gradualness of Bukharin's approach. Bukharin had argued that the peasants should 'enrich themselves' and 'ride into socialism on a peasant nag': he held that the peasant–worker *smychka* should be maintained. This was the position that Lenin had adopted with the NEP, so Bukharin could justifiably argue that this was the proper Leninist line to take; but Stalin now believed it was time to break with the NEP. It had certainly been a success in bringing stability to the war-ravaged economy, as the country returned to its pre-First World War levels of growth, and many peasants had attained a better standard of living, but this had been achieved by forcing workers to work in conditions similar to those they had experienced before the revolution. Workers declared that the NEP was nothing more than the 'New Exploitation of the Proletariat'.

Stalin's desire to break with the gradualness of the NEP suggests that he was more in tune with the mood of the party than people like Bukharin. Many workers felt betrayed and believed that the promises of the October Revolution had not been fulfilled; they began to demand more radical measures to hasten the move to socialism. Stalin amalgamated the Left and Right platforms, taking ideas from both. From the Left he took the policy of rapid industrialisation, which would appeal to those workers who wanted socialism to be built much more quickly; from the Right he took the idea of 'Socialism in One Country'. This galvanised the Russian workers, who recognised that the revolution had failed to spread internationally and was unlikely to do so in the near future. In 1927, the international situation became more unstable: first the British Conservative government broke off diplomatic relations with the Kremlin and then thousands of Chinese Communists were massacred by Chiang Kai-shek's Nationalists. Stalin felt that hostile capitalist forces were encircling the Soviet Union, and so he pursued a more nationalist policy than Trotsky, or indeed Lenin, had wanted.

Slow domestic progress and the threatening international situation combined to present Stalin with an excellent opportunity to position himself to win the leadership campaign. Building on the decision taken at the Fifteenth Party Congress in 1927 for an ambitious industrial programme, Stalin announced a more aggressive and coercive policy to requisition grain from the peasants. The Right Opposition claimed that this went against what Lenin had wanted and accused Stalin of betrayal. Stalin's reaction gave some clues to the kind of system he was building: he simply used his position in the party to remove his opponents and their supporters from their positions in the Central Committee and the trade unions. By 1929 any member supporting the Right Opposition had been removed from the leadership. Stalin was now first among equals.

The reasons for the defeat of the Right Opposition were similar to those that had brought about the downfall of the Left. The Right's leaders had failed to take into account the changing international situation. While the Left did not realise that the revolution was unlikely to spread, the Right ignored the worsening relations with other countries which created the hostile international environment that made rapid industrialisation appear so necessary. As proponents of gradualist and pro-peasant policies, the Right had little to offer workers who were desperate for the radical socialist changes that they had been promised in 1917.

Conclusion

At the start of the 1920s, the Communist Party was led by Vladimir Il'ich Lenin and was looking to establish a socialist system through gradualist policies that relied on an alliance between workers and peasants. After Lenin's death in 1924, Leon Trotsky seemed to be the most obvious choice to take control of the party, but by the end of the decade, the Communists were led by Josef Stalin and had embarked upon a radical programme of industrialisation and collectivisation that would smash Lenin's *smychka*. Democratic debate had been stifled within the party and factions were banned. Although this had occurred under Lenin, Stalin used it to manoeuvre himself and his supporters into the most powerful positions.

Whether Stalin had long-term plans to lead the party at the start of the 1920s is debatable. However, he certainly made the most of the opportunities that were presented to him, from the ban on factions to the weaknesses and mistakes of his opponents. These factors combined with specific socioeconomic and political conditions to allow Stalin to make use of his support within the party. They suggest that there was more to Stalin's successful rise to power than just an individual's ruthless desire for control. It may even be claimed that, at the specific moment when he broke with Bukharin, Stalin more than anyone else reflected a genuine desire from the lower ranks of the party for more radical policies. Whether Stalin represented the real Leninist tradition, however, is highly questionable.

Questions

1 To what extent was Lenin to blame for Stalin's rise?
2 What was the rationale behind the Cult of Lenin?
3 What were the main factors that enabled Stalin to wrong-foot both Left and Right Oppositions?

The Stalinist economy: a means of control?

At the end of the 1920s Stalin began his 'Revolution from Above'. This was a huge restructuring of the Soviet economy that saw millions of workers embark on the industrialisation of the country, while peasants were forced to work the land in collective farms. A socialist economy was ushered in, with central planning replacing the vagaries of the free market, which allowed the USSR to weather the storm of the Great Depression that hit the West after the Wall Street Crash in 1929. The Communist Party began to organise society through agencies such as Gosplan (State Committee for Planning) and *Vesenkha* (Supreme Council of the National Economy). It was the start of a new era in Russian and world history: the Soviet government was the first administration specifically set up to plan for the economic needs of its people. Stalin launched a Five-Year Plan in 1928 to create the kind of 'material abundance' that Karl Marx had assumed would follow after the socialist revolution. The Five-Year Plan (*pyatiletka*) sought to organise the needs of society through economic decision-making: moving peasants onto collective farms made it even more imperative to modernise their agricultural techniques once they got there.

By the end of the 1930s the country had finally been dragged into the twentieth century. Peasants exchanged horse-drawn ploughs for mechanised tractors; huge new cities such as Magnitogorsk in the Ural Mountains were thrown up, and the Soviet Union industrialised on a massive scale. But the 'great turn' brought with it equally great oppression: workers had their right to movement within the country restricted and came under pressure to fulfil the ridiculously high targets of the Five-Year Plan. The collectivisation process saw peasants herded onto collective farms against their will and provoked famine in Ukraine and southern Russia that left millions dead: indeed, some scholars have argued that the famine was a deliberate act by Stalin to crush the peasantry. What was Stalin's motivation for these great socioeconomic changes? Were the harsh measures taken by the government during industrialisation and collectivisation really necessary for the implementation of Soviet socialism, or did Stalin simply use this rapid change as a means of controlling the population?

The need for industrialisation

A forced industrialisation programme was always highly likely, regardless of who became leader after Lenin. The debates in the 1920s did not focus on whether or not the USSR should industrialise but on how quickly it should do so. The basic starting point for all party members was that industrialisation was ideologically necessary since, according to their Marxist understanding of the world, this was the only way to build a socialist society. The Left called for rapid restructuring while the Right wanted to take a more gradual approach.

By the late 1920s, the international situation had become more threatening, and Soviet workers had grown disillusioned with the country's slow progress towards socialism. They were also dissatisfied with the way the peasants appeared to be gaining far more from the NEP than they were. The workers were the Communist Party's natural supporters, yet they saw the NEP's limited return of capitalism only in terms of its bad features: sackings, unemployment, 'bourgeois decadence' and corruption. The NEP appeared to be coming to a natural end and there was no longer the desire, from the Stalinists at least, to help it continue. An ideological response that favoured the working class was badly needed: this was one of the main reasons why Stalin launched the industrialisation programme.

The unstable international situation prompted Stalin to claim that there were many external enemies who wanted to destroy the Soviet Union. He also claimed that anti-Soviet elements were active within Soviet borders, an allegation that created a new, suspicious atmosphere, made worse by the Shakhty Affair of May 1928. The security police claimed that they had uncovered a counter-revolutionary plot involving technical specialists and foreign powers at the Shakhty mines in the Donbass industrial complex in southern Russia. Fifty-three engineers, including three from Germany, were accused of 'wrecking' equipment, committing sabotage and maintaining links with the former capitalist owners of the coalmines. The truth was rather different: foreign equipment had been misused and this had caused fires to break out in the mines. This was not uncommon, as semi-skilled workers often found it difficult to work new machines, but the difference in this case was that the regime deliberately used these mistakes as a weapon against 'class enemies'. There was a public trial in Moscow and a press campaign demanding 'Death to the Wreckers!' Some of the accused were forced to confess to the charges: some did so in part, while others tried to retract their confessions. Eleven death sentences were pronounced and five were carried out.

This change in the political atmosphere at home and abroad contributed significantly to the launching of Stalin's 'Revolution from Above'. Derogatory terms such as 'wrecker' were introduced into Soviet vocabulary, becoming common usage in the 1930s. Stalinist rhetoric inspired the notion that, while there might be enemies everywhere, they would prove no match for the Communists. Soviet terminology constantly alluded to an ongoing war against the capitalists; phrases such as 'socialist offensive' and slogans such as 'There are no fortresses Bolsheviks cannot storm' were employed to remind citizens that they were all part of the class struggle. Whether these enemies were real or imaginary, Stalin used the opportunity to prioritise heavy industry and build up Soviet military strength. However, this came at the expense of consumer goods, so Marx's dream of the material abundance that would end the hunger and poverty of capitalism took an early blow.

Industrialisation was also launched because the Soviet Union was economically 'backward' when compared with other major powers such as Britain and the USA. The Communist Party was concerned that the USSR was surrounded by strong, hostile enemies. Rapid industrialisation seemed the only way to ensure its safety. In November 1929 Stalin addressed the question of Russian 'backwardness', saying that Soviet Russia was becoming a country of metal, automobiles and tractors. In 1931 he declared that the tempo of Soviet industrialisation could not be slackened: the Soviet Union was 'fifty to a hundred years behind' the capitalist powers of Britain and the USA and the USSR had to catch up or else 'they will crush us'.

There were two important messages in Stalin's statements. The first was that the USSR would no longer feel threatened by the capitalist West once the industrialisation drive had been successful. The second was that it was imperative for the USSR to overtake the West, and this competitive element became an important theme in East–West relations. However, the need for speed and rapid reconstruction in the early 1930s meant that it would be difficult to be too concerned with the human cost. This lack of compassion or care for the suffering of the Soviet people became characteristic of Stalin's rule.

Stalin was also motivated in this drive for industrialisation by his belief in a great and powerful Soviet Union, even though this 'Great Russian chauvinism' contradicted his Bolshevik ideals. He did not hesitate to invoke memories of strong tsars from pre-Communist times, such as Ivan IV ('Ivan the Terrible') and Peter the Great, the modernising tsar. Stalin thought that they had merely done what was necessary to ensure Russia's security and greatness. Industrialisation was also driven by the demand from workers impatient with Russia's slow progress towards socialism. It was not introduced specifically as a means of control; however, as we shall see, state control was a consequence of the fact that the plan was implemented by a Stalinist bureaucracy staffed with people more concerned with protecting their own positions than with creating a socialist society.

Why collectivise?

Collectivisation of Soviet agriculture was a necessary partner of Soviet industrialisation: it would have been impossible for the country to function with a modernised industrial basis but an outdated agricultural sector. The NEP had largely come to an end by 1928 and some believed it had fulfilled what it set out to do, namely to stabilise the Soviet economy until the party could launch the 'socialist offensive' in agriculture. The start of the industrialisation project also meant that the leadership had to turn its attention to how it would ensure enough food reached the workers in the cities. Collectivisation was therefore the second — and essential — part of the Communists' programme of constructing socialism in the USSR.

As with industrialisation, although there was a consensus on the need for change in agriculture, disagreements emerged over the correct way to proceed. Aleksei Rykov and Mikhail Kalinin favoured a cautious approach, while Stalin and Molotov were more hostile towards the kulaks: Stalin later said that he wanted to liquidate the kulaks as a class. Collectivisation was clearly ideologically desirable, as it would ensure that peasants worked for the good of the whole economy rather than for their own personal gain. A socialised economy means more than simply bringing the means of production under state control: there has to be a definite shift in the reasons why people produce goods in the first place. The problem was that Stalinism neglected the needs of the individual; in the post-NEP Soviet Union the health of the whole community and of the state took precedence over individual needs.

Towards the end of the 1920s procuring grain became a problem. The Soviet government reduced the price it paid, but this led to peasant resistance; the *smychka* was beginning to break down. Stalin believed the problem was caused by kulaks hoarding their grain supplies and claimed they were holding the regime to ransom. He visited Siberia to see things for himself and, convinced that the kulaks were to blame, told officials to find more food at the same low prices. This became known as the Urals-Siberian method and involved grain seizures, arresting kulaks and attempting to force peasants onto collective farms. Bukharin attacked Stalin for destroying the links between town and country, worker and peasant, but Stalin took a pragmatic line, insisting that cheap grain was necessary for the success of industrialisation and to ensure that there were enough supplies to feed the workers and fulfil the country's export quotas.

Stalin's pragmatism can be interpreted as an extension of state control over the peasantry, a large section of society which was not a natural ally of the Communists. Stalin was deeply suspicious of the peasants, and it has been argued by Robert Conquest that this suspicion led to a politically inspired campaign designed to crush the peasantry and increase the power of the Communist Party. According to Conquest, this was part of Stalin's totalitarian design to subordinate the population to himself and to the party. Conquest also focused on the Ukrainian famine (discussed below) which he termed a 'terror famine'.

This is one of the clearest arguments supporting the idea that the Stalinist economy was a means of control, especially over the peasantry. However, less extreme assessments than Conquest's focus not so much on Stalin's apparent desire for total control as on the political and economic situation at the end of the 1920s, asking whether Stalin had any realistic alternative to forced collect-ivisation. According to Alec Nove and R. W. Davies, the ways in which the party perceived problems such as peasant resistance to grain procurements had more to do with ensuring that workers in the cities had enough food than it did with Stalin's need for total personal control. Nove argues that while there were alter-natives open to Stalin, his decisions need to be understood within their political and economic context. By the late 1920s the USSR was economically weak and largely isolated internationally, which only increased the sense of insecurity in the Kremlin. In the Bolsheviks' understanding, shaped in part during the harsh Civil War years, the world was full of class enemies eager to counter the Communist threat. Moreover, many members had only joined the party during or after the Civil War and were considered politically suspect. More careerist elements had replaced some of the more 'ideologically sound' workers who had died protecting the gains of the revolution. These new party members inter-preted problems in crude ideological terms, so that the Kremlin now saw the grain procurement problem as a political rather than economic question. They interpreted it as resistance from their class enemies and, according to Nove, they thought a harsh policy was necessary to ensure access to the grain supply.

R. W. Davies claims that despite the grain crisis, even as late as 1929 Stalin was still unsure about what to do; however, the changing political situation helped him to make up his mind by the time of that year's plenum of the Central Committee. While there was concern about the onset of industrialisa-tion, there was also excitement about the growth of 'voluntary' collectivisation, which had been achieved by local activists with only limited use of force. Stalin and his comrades saw this as an extension of the class conflict into the coun-tryside and took it as an indication of support for their agricultural policy. Stalin now believed that if the party pressed ahead with collectivisation it would meet with less opposition.

Nove and Davies differ from Conquest in that they concentrate less on Stalin the person and more on the development of his policies within the socio-political and economic context of the time. Other arguments focus on the level of support for collectivisation among those who lived in the cities. This support for Stalin's policies is discussed in more detail in Chapter 5, but it is worth noting here that thousands of activists went from the towns to the country to spread Communist ideas. This was done with an almost religious zeal, and it followed an old Russian tradition of city people taking a modernising message out 'to the people' in the countryside. Inspired by the defeat of the Right Opposition, many party workers, known as 'twenty-five-thousanders' (because the party decreed that 25,000 industrial workers should go to the villages), voluntarily went to the countryside to offer their technical expertise to help improve the performance of the *kolkhoz* (collective farm). The year 1929 became the time of the 'Great Breakthrough' and articles in newspapers such as *Pravda* called for an expansion of the collective farms and an offensive against rural capitalists. The collectivisation drive was in full flow.

The problem with Stalin's 'Revolution from Above' approach to socialism was that it provoked confrontation with different groups, most noticeably the peasantry. There may have been support inside the party for the rapid modern-isation of the Soviet system, but there was much less support for the means by which it would be achieved. There was little dialogue between party, workers and peasants, the very opposite of what many believed should happen in a genuinely socialist economy; instead Soviet industrialisation was built on coercion and slave labour. Politically suspect peasants, the so-called 'kulaks' and criminals worked alongside free workers, but they did so within the empire of prison camps known as the gulag. Coercive methods were also used to crush any peasant resistance to being moved onto the collective farms.

It is to the course of the Plan and its consequences that we now turn. We shall see that a controlling instinct developed in Moscow when dealing with the provinces. But was this because of Stalin's 'natural desire' to control everything, or because poor implementation of policy by regional party bosses forced the centre to intervene more than it might otherwise have done? It was a mixture of both.

Industrialisation and control

The Five-Year Plan set targets for industries to achieve. If individual ministries failed to reach their targets, party and factory bosses found their positions, and often their freedom, under threat. One consequence was that intense competi-tion for resources developed between the different factories and ministries. This made for confusion, panic and improvisation: Stalin's Plan suffered from a severe lack of coordination.

The effects of industrialisation outside the workplace also created problems. Workers could be forced to move around the country to fill gaps in the labour force, and the conditions they met were often as bad as the very worst excesses of nineteenth-century industrialisation, thanks both to the rapid tempo of Soviet reconstruction and to Stalin's blatant disregard for human life. The human cost of this revolution from above was extraordinarily high and in many areas the loss of life, combined with threats and coercion, created a climate of fear. In this way, Stalin's economic policies can be interpreted as a means of control, in that they placed great emphasis on restricting the freedoms of Soviet citizens.

The most obvious form of repression was the gulag, the vast network of forced labour camps where innocent people were forced to work for the state. Ordinary citizens became victims of harsh new labour laws which, for example, criminalised unauthorised food consumption, while many peasants were the victims of large-scale deportations. Gulag inmates were often put to work on heavy industrial projects such as canal-building; tens of thousands of prisoners died during the construction of the infamous White Sea Canal. These huge projects required a vast labour pool, which could be found in the gulag. After 1934 Stalin's secret police force, the NKVD (People's Commissariat for Internal Affairs), took control of the camps. The growth in numbers of inmates who were forced to work on the industrialisation project in the early 1930s coincided with a tightening of the Soviet labour code, which governed workers' rights and conditions. The camps now had an economic as well as political role: prisoners could 'learn' that the common good was everything, and 'correction through labour' became the gulag's ideological justification.

Industrialisation concentrated primarily on the growth of heavy industry, such as steel, coal and machine tools, in what became known as the Cult of Metal, led, of course, by Stalin, the self-styled 'man of steel'. Reducing consumption to the bare minimum allowed the government greater investment in heavy industry and defence, though at the expense of light industry. The low priority given to consumer goods meant poor general welfare for many workers, who were often seen less as human beings than as cogs in a huge productionist machine. Workers were forced to live in awful conditions: new arrivals at Moscow's electricity works were sent to a long wooden hut, where beds without blankets or pillows were crowded side by side and had to be shared in shifts. Families were often squeezed into 'communal apartments', usually pre-war single-family flats divided up with a family to each room and a communal kitchen, bathroom and toilet. Sometimes not even a room could be spared to house a family. In the new industrial town of Magnitogorsk in the Urals, which had been no more than a village before industrialisation, workers lived in tents

until more permanent houses were built. But the need for rapid and vast industrialisation was great and saw the creation of whole new industrial areas, such
as the hydroelectric power station on the Dnepr River or the huge new tractor
factories in Stalingrad, Chelyabinsk and Kharkov. This enormous level of
investment in the Soviet infrastructure also saw a massive mobilisation of
under-utilised labour: there was significant population movement from rural
to urban areas, and on average towns grew by 50,000 people a week.

The Soviet state now became much more involved in people's lives, yet in
many ways the system was more improvised than successfully planned. There
was a general sense of fear of the consequences of failing to achieve the set
targets: factory managers did anything they could to ensure that they fulfilled
or even overfulfilled the Plan, and as moderation became politically suspect,
haste and arbitrariness became commonplace. The targets set by Moscow were
often wildly unrealistic, so managers falsified their figures, lying about how
much they had produced. The fear of what would happen to them if they failed
to deliver — perhaps losing their position or else being sent to the gulag — was
an underlying force that drove the economy and acted as a subconscious means
of control.

Enterprise managers were often forced to compete to survive. Lorries were
hijacked and supply trains ambushed as bosses tried desperately to ensure that
their targets were met; some simply commandeered supplies intended for rival
managers. As a result, there was little cooperation in a system that was supposed
to be establishing a planned socialist economy. In some ways the system still
retained a capitalist element in this competition for resources between rival
factories and ministries; with no possibility of guaranteeing resources the whole
system sometimes became highly arbitrary. So, while it may be difficult to argue
that socialism was being constructed, it is not hard to see that a controlled
economy was developing as a direct consequence of Stalin's declared need for
speed.

By the early 1930s Stalinist control over the economy was widespread but far
from total, as is demonstrated by the level of resistance in the towns and countryside. Strikes and worker-led resistance spread to regions to the south and east
of Moscow. The Ivanovo industrial region, the Urals and the Lower Volga were
just some of the places where workers criticised officials, refused to operate
machinery or openly demonstrated against the poor living conditions.
Thousands participated in violent strikes which party leaders in Moscow interpreted as a rise in anti-Communist activity by class enemies, although these
actions were more concerned with the poor conditions, especially the severe lack
of food, than with bringing down the Stalinist dictatorship. The strikes were
never referred to publicly in the press or directly in speeches, but they allowed

the party to claim that 'bourgeois' elements were still active in the country. This was a typical Stalinist response, ignoring the actual causes of the problems and instead choosing to see 'class enemies', 'saboteurs' and 'wreckers' at work. The strikes undoubtedly contributed to Stalin's move for even greater control in the economy and the country as a whole; 'anti-party' action could not and would not be tolerated; but the strikes and other worker-led resistance highlight the fact that total control in a country the size of the USSR would always be extremely difficult to achieve.

The workers' strikes were a significant reminder to some in the Communist Party that the Stalinist path was not the only way forward and they led some members of the Central Committee to question Stalin's policies of industrialisation and collectivisation. The widespread devastation in the countryside and the strikes by the party's natural supporters in the towns came as a sharp reminder that oppressive tactics often provoke resistance. These moves also challenge the 'totalitarian' interpretation of the all-controlling Stalin: anti-Stalinist activity was still very much a part of Soviet culture in the early 1930s.

Collectivisation: mastering the peasantry

There is no denying that Stalin's agricultural policies involved waging war on the peasants. 'Kulaks' were demonised and for a while became Class Enemy Number One. Stalin made no effort to hide his desire to destroy the kulaks as a class by putting an end to their economic activities and by so breaking them that they could not pose a collective threat. He was not particularly concerned if this process also entailed mass murder in the countryside.

The official definition of a kulak came to be a person who employed another person for more than 50 days per year; however, this definition was progressively expanded by official decrees. In February 1930 a decree divided kulaks into three classes: counter-revolutionaries, exploiters and active opponents of the regime, and the economically powerful: each had a different fate. Counter-revolutionaries were executed or exiled and their property was confiscated; exploiters and active opponents were deported but retained some possessions; the economically powerful were allowed to remain in the locality but suffered confiscation of their property and were not allowed to join the collective farms. This caused great confusion: many non-kulaks were denounced and deported by mistake. This was sometimes done deliberately by people with a grudge; at other times it happened when party workers who had gone to work in the countryside let their revolutionary zeal get in the way of clear and objective judgement. Anyone suspected of resisting grain deliveries or who opposed joining the collective farms could be labelled a kulak. In some places the confusion over what exactly was supposed to be collectivised was such that over-zealous party members actually confiscated the clothes the peasants were wearing. The class war was now visiting the countryside with a vengeance.

There was great resistance to Moscow's agricultural plans in rural areas and peasants struggled against the implementation of the party's ideas. They slaughtered their livestock and gorged their grain rather than hand it over to officials. Peasants even set fire to their homes rather than surrender them to the state. By March 1930 the countryside was in chaos; officials were often forced to improvise in a climate of enthusiasm and haste.

To help calm the situation, Stalin called for a temporary lull in the collectivisation drive and *Pravda* published an article written by the Soviet leader entitled 'Dizzy with Success' in which he called for a return to voluntary collectivisation, whereby the peasants willingly moved onto collective farms without the use of force. He blamed the over-enthusiasm of party workers for the misery and upheaval that disturbed the peasants' lives and implied that they had gone too far in their desire to collectivise everything. This temporary lull led to a sharp fall in the numbers of peasants who remained on the collective farms; this exodus is a reminder that where the peasants were concerned, coercion was a conscious policy pursued by the Stalinist dictatorship.

After this lull, the socialist offensive was resumed: in late 1930 pressure was put on the peasants to move onto the collective farms. Those who held back were given inferior land to farm and higher grain quotas to fulfil. State control was maintained by the local party organisations, the OGPU (United State Political Administration — the secret police) and the Machine Tractor Stations (MTS), which had initially been established to oversee the application of new technology but became a useful means of political control as well. Each collective farm had an MTS and, until 1934, a political department. These bodies kept watch over activities on the farms. They were run by the political director of the MTS, but with an OGPU representative attached to them too. Police agents acted as Moscow's eyes and ears and were there to ensure that party orders were obeyed. Central control was maintained by the local party committee or the rural soviet, so collectives enjoyed little freedom or independence. Central control also involved coercive legislation, criminalising unauthorised food consumption (November 1931), making the theft of grain from *kolkhoz* fields punishable by death (August 1932), and reintroducing the old tsarist internal passports to prevent workers and peasants moving to towns in search of food (December 1932).

Forced collectivisation resulted in an improvement in the 1930 harvest compared with that of the previous year and 90% collectivisation of farms by 1936; by contrast, Lenin's voluntary socialisation of the land had brought less than 1% of the rural population into the collective sector. However, between 1932 and 1933 there was a catastrophic famine in Ukraine, southern Russia and the Caucasus, which led to such a huge loss of life that it took until 1938 for the USSR to regain the production levels it had reached in 1928. Approximately 1 million 'kulak' families were driven out of their homes or died either protecting their property or on the long journey into exile. Whole villages were wiped out and there were rumours that desperate people were driven to cannibalism. The overall death rate is now said to have been approximately 5 million people, with the weakest members of society being affected the most.

The Soviet authorities kept stories of the suffering out of the Soviet press and tried to hide the consequences of the famine from their citizens: not only would the details have contradicted official propaganda about the success of Soviet socialism, but hostile foreign powers could have seen the famine as evidence that the Soviet Union was in crisis and turned it to their advantage.

Stalin's hand in this catastrophic devastation is clear: his demands for rapid collectivisation caused much of the large-scale havoc. However, Robert Conquest's claim that this was a 'terror-famine', a deliberate attempt by Stalin to suppress rising Ukrainian nationalism or to crush peasant opposition to collectivisation, has been challenged by historians such as R. W. Davies, Mark Tauger and Geoffrey Wheatcroft. They have questioned Conquest's assertion that the Stalinist government deliberately withheld vast grain reserves that might have lessened the devastating consequences of the famine. With the benefit of archival evidence, they argue that there simply was not enough extra food for starving peasants. Indeed, there was barely enough to feed the Red Army, at a time when the country was preparing for possible war after Japan's invasion of Manchuria in 1931. Stalin 'was not hoarding immense grain reserves', argues Davies, because he had 'failed to reach the levels he had been…demanding since 1929' (Davies et al., in C. Reed 2003, p. 100).

Although Stalin did not believe the peasants' protestations that they did not have the grain to fulfil their quotas, the Kremlin finally learned the truth from police reports in late 1932 and early 1933. It may have been far too late to do anything to alleviate the suffering, but it is significant that such high requisitioning targets were not ordered again. Conquest's argument rests on Stalin's personal wickedness, as the totalitarian school of thought often does; but seeing the famine simply as a Stalinist plot to suppress Ukrainian nationalism ignores the fact that the famine spread beyond Ukraine into southern Russia and the Caucasus. A more plausible, though no less disturbing, explanation is a combination of the incompetence of the Soviet authorities, who saw only 'kulak sabotage', Stalin's own mistrust of the peasantry, his desire to collectivise quickly and his blatant disregard for human life. Stalin cannot be judged blameless in any way, but it is difficult to argue that the famine and the terrible consequences of his haphazard agricultural policy were deliberately masterminded as a way of gaining total control over the country.

Conclusion

Once the leaders in the Kremlin had decided to launch the industrialisation and collectivisation programmes, a centrally planned economy inevitably followed. However, while the need for central planning stemmed from Communist ideology, the drive for central control grew out of the need to ensure that policies emanating from Moscow were implemented properly throughout the country. This is not to say that Stalin did not want power, but he did not set the USSR on the path of modernisation simply as a means of gaining control over the population. Extensive central control and strict discipline were consequences of the poor implementation of the Five-Year Plan as much as of Stalin's controlling personality. At the start of the first Plan, direction from the centre was necessary; by the end of it, central direction had turned into overt control of the population.

Questions

1 What does Stalin's use of 'Great Russian chauvinism' to promote the Five-Year Plans suggest about the political beliefs of the Soviet people?
2 How fair is it to see collectivisation essentially as an exercise in social engineering?
3 Did the modernisation of the Soviet Union have to involve so much fear and violence?

Reference

● Davies, R. W., et al. (2003) 'Stalin, Grain Stocks and the Famine of 1932–1933' in C. Read (ed.) *The Stalin Years: A Reader*, Palgrave Macmillan.

Chapter 4

1932: a tyrant born?

In the early 1930s Stalin consolidated his power in the Communist Party. Not only did he become head of the party, and therefore head of the Soviet Union, but he became virtually untouchable. The signs were already visible at the celebrations for his fiftieth birthday in 1929, when the word *vozhd'* was first used to describe him. *Vozhd'* means 'leader', with connotations similar to those of Führer, the title adopted by Hitler. During this period the Communist Party as a collective institution declined in importance while the position of General Secretary became all-important and the OGPU became Stalin's personal police force, ensuring that the dictatorship of the party became Stalin's personal dictatorship.

Stalin's rule can be characterised in various ways, all of which emphasise his power as a politician and leader, although not necessarily as a Communist. Apart from the obvious 'dictator' label, Stalin can be seen as a mafia boss surrounded by henchmen. He could certainly offer a privileged life to those who gave him unconditional loyalty, or take it away at any time if they opposed him. Many of Stalin's old comrades fell victim as he followed through their removal from power to its ultimate, fatal conclusion. Stalin ruled the Communist Party according to a strict code of honour whereby insults had to be avenged no matter how long it took. He had a very long memory, reaching back 20 years or more to when someone had crossed him; it did not matter whether it had been a relatively minor disagreement over policy or a major threat to Stalin's power, such as Trotsky's alliance with Zinoviev and Kamenev. Stalin was the Godfather to an entire nation and had power of life and death not only over those close to him but over millions of people.

Stalin can also be seen as the chief oligarch at the head of a political system run by a small but powerful group of people. This was far removed from the socialist dream of an inclusive system that encouraged popular participation. It may even be said that he was the arch-ruler of the new Soviet ruling class or aristocracy (*znat'*), a tsar-like figure. When his mother asked him in 1935, 'Josef, what exactly are you now?' he replied, 'Remember the tsar? I'm something like a tsar.' His mother's response was that he would have done better to have become a priest. No doubt millions of peasants would have agreed.

Of course, Soviet citizens knew little of these alternative 'Stalins': images that portrayed him as anything less than a great leader and Lenin's natural heir were carefully airbrushed from history. It was in this era that the 'Cult of Stalin' began, starting with the use of the word *vozhd'* and continuing with the invention of the term 'Stalinism', coined by the Stalin loyalist Lazar Kaganovich. The Stalin cult ensured that the *vozhd'* was officially represented as the people's friend and saviour, rather than as a mafia 'godfather' with the power of life and death over countless innocents in his hands.

The year 1932 marked a key stage in the process that saw Stalin become dictator, oligarch or tsar. This was the year when he eliminated the remaining internal opposition to him and his policies. Even though Stalin had won the power struggle in the 1920s there were still some who openly disagreed with him, such as Sergei Syrtsov, Vissarion Lominadze, and Martemyan Ryutin, author of a 200-page appeal to his comrades calling for a less harsh approach to be taken in the countryside. Although this was a secret document, it became known as the 'Ryutin platform'. The manner in which Stalin was forced to deal with these remaining opponents was important. The Politburo blocked his demands for them to be shot, an indication that he did not yet have total domination of the party. Within just a few years, however, the party had been purged of any remaining opposition, with many of those purged being shot. This says much about how Stalin's power within the party had changed.

This was also a year of great personal tragedy for Stalin, as his second wife, Nadya Alliluyeva, committed suicide. He showed the raw emotions of any human being who has lost a great love. His cold belief in the forces of history that allowed him to ignore the suffering in the countryside during collectivisation momentarily washed away; it has been suggested that this tragic incident may have been a turning point in his personal life. His nephew Leonid Redens even claimed that Nadya's suicide 'altered history' and made the Great Terror later in the decade inevitable. According to Redens's account Stalin lost all inhibitions after Nadya's death. Although it is too simplistic to suggest that widespread mass murder was the direct result of Stalin's personal loss, Nadya's suicide did influence his behaviour and perhaps extinguished any spark of human emotion that she might have reignited in his heart.

Defeating challenges to power

It was in this early period of Soviet history that Stalin began to relegate the Communist Party to a less important position. It retained its leading role in the USSR, but Stalin and his close allies moved into an ever stronger position at the expense of leading organisations, including the Politburo. In 1930 Sergei Syrtsov, newly appointed to this body, was shocked to discover that the Politburo he thought he knew 'was a fiction. Everything is really decided behind the Politburo's back by a small clique....' Arguably, the process began in 1930 with the defeat of the challenge to Stalin's policies from Syrtsov and Lominadze, and it took an important turn in Stalin's favour in 1932 with the end of the Ryutin platform and the 'anti-party' group of Smirnov, Eismont and Tolmachev. It is to these political challenges to Stalin's position that we now turn.

Strains and cracks began to show in the Communist hierarchy in 1930 as collectivisation took hold of the countryside, although an organised opposition was not yet established. Some Communists below the top level of the party, led by Syrtsov and Lominadze, disagreed with Stalin's harsh policy and called for a different approach. They had to do this privately, as factions had been banned by Lenin in 1921 and the party was demonstrating, publicly at least, unanimous support for its leader and his policies.

Syrtsov was Chairman of the Council of People's Commissars of the Russian Republic, a full member of the Central Committee and a candidate member of the Politburo between 1929 and 1930. Lominadze was also a Central Committee member and head of the Transcaucasian party organisation. They originally sided with Stalin against Bukharin but grew profoundly shocked at what was happening in the Soviet countryside. This inspired them to seek support for a change of policy, including an end to the campaign of forced collectivisation, and even to question whether Stalin's policies would in fact lead the country to socialism. Syrtsov spoke of the problems of 'extraordinary centralisation' and 'rampant bureaucratism', which could be seen as a Trotskyist critique, while Lominadze denounced the regime's questionable attitude towards Soviet workers and peasants.

The opinions and demands of these Communists were easily suppressed by Stalin: they were denounced as 'right oppositionists' and 'double-dealers', saying one thing and doing another, and removed from their posts. The important thing to note, however, is that there was criticism of Stalinist tactics in the higher echelons of the Communist Party: bitterness towards the General Secretary and his apparent lack of concern for the people of the Soviet Union was no longer the preserve of the exploited masses. Syrtsov and Lominadze's campaign to change the party's direction failed and both men lost their high party positions: Lominadze was appointed Party Secretary at the new Magnitogorsk power station and Syrtsov was moved to various positions in state-owned enterprises. Their campaign against Stalin sealed their long-term fates: both were purged and executed later in the decade.

The fact that Syrtsov and Lominadze lost their roles in top-level Soviet politics did not deter others from challenging the policies of Stalin and his entourage. In 1932 there were two more attempts to remove him. The first came from

Martemyan Ryutin, who had supported Bukharin's challenge to Stalin's agricultural extremism and had been district secretary of the Moscow party organisation. The second came from Aleksandr Smirnov, Vladimir Tolmachev and Nikolai Eismont, who made up an informal anti-Stalin group.

Ryutin's resistance to Stalin began in early 1932, when he worked with a small group of Bukharin's supporters to draft and circulate in secret the 200-page paper 'Stalin and the Crisis of the Proletarian Dictatorship', which represented the so-called 'Ryutin platform'. This attack on Stalin reflected the former Right Opposition's stance, calling Stalin the 'evil genius of the Russian Revolution' and claiming he was vindictive and driven by a 'lust for power'. Ryutin held that Stalin and his clique were destroying the Communist cause: his paper stated that Stalin had 'brought the revolution to the edge of the abyss'. This was a stunning assault on the 'Boss', and Ryutin followed it up with an 'Appeal to All Party Members', which he edited with a dozen other comrades in an apartment in the Moscow suburbs. This fact highlights the secret nature of this oppositionist adventure: there was no way that anyone who was calling for the removal of Stalin and his 'clique' could do so openly until they could be sure of widespread support.

As well as demanding the removal of Stalin and criticising the General Secretary personally, the Ryutin platform called for an economic retreat, the end of forced collectivisation and the rehabilitation of oppositionists — including Stalin's arch-enemy, Trotsky. Ryutin's paper also called for party members to oppose Stalin's policies and requested that the document be read, copied and then passed on. It is difficult to know how widely read the document was, but copies were circulated in cities as far apart as Moscow and Kharkov, 400 miles away. Stalin certainly knew about it — a copy was found in his wife's room at the time of her death — and he took the call to 'destroy Stalin's dictatorship' to mean his forced removal through armed revolt.

Although Ryutin's document was intended to be read by other oppositionists, the clandestine nature of this opposition meant that it was difficult to know who should receive copies. The consequence was that the document soon fell into the hands of the OGPU; the arrests of Ryutin and his supporters began in September. All were expelled from the party and sentenced to imprisonment for being members of a 'counter-revolutionary organisation'. Boris Nikolaevsky's *Letter of an Old Bolshevik*, published in 1936 after a meeting with Bukharin in Paris, claimed that Stalin was so angry that he demanded the death penalty for these oppositionists but was blocked by other members of the Politburo. Kirov was the first to speak up against the death penalty for Ryutin: he said that Ryutin was 'not a lost man but an errant one' and that 'people would not understand us' if he was shot. Instead Ryutin was given a 10-year prison term, although this made little difference in the long run: he and other members of the platform were purged and shot in 1937. By the end of 1932, other former oppositionist leaders including Kamenev, Zinoviev and Karl Radek had been called before party disciplinary bodies to be questioned about their possible connection to the group and whether they had read Ryutin's document or were aware of the platform. Knowing about the platform and not informing the relevant authorities soon came to be regarded as a crime.

The final threat to the ruling Stalinist elite came from a small group of government administrators led by Eismont, Tolmachev and Smirnov. These men had been members of the party for decades: Smirnov had been Central Committee secretary and Agriculture Commissar between 1928 and 1930. They were well placed to understand what the party stood for and the reality of what it was now doing. They called for Stalin's removal as well as for independent trade unions, the dissolution of most collective farms and the transfer of control of the secret police from Stalin to the party. These oppositionist activities got Smirnov expelled from the Central Committee and the Orgburo and the others thrown out of the party. Smirnov's lighter punishment may have been because he was not actually present at the meeting in Eismont's apartment when this 'anti-party' group discussed replacing Stalin; nevertheless, his closeness to those who were present earned him a stark warning that his continued party membership depended on his future behaviour. At the Central Committee plenum in January 1933 Smirnov 'resolutely and categorically' denied the 'vile, counter-revolutionary words concerning Comrade Stalin' that were attributed to him by someone who was at the Eismont gathering. He was expelled from the party a year later for 'double-dealing' and arrested and shot during the purging of the party in 1937. Tolmachev was arrested in 1933 and Eismont was arrested in 1932 and sentenced to 3 years in the labour camps. He was released in 1935 but died in a car accident shortly afterwards.

Consolidating power

These examples of opposition to Stalin in the higher echelons of the party are evidence that Stalin still did not have complete command of the Communist Party even in the early 1930s, though he was moving into a position where he could take more power. The year 1932 may be seen as a key stage in Stalin's rise to the position of 'first among equals'. The process was concluded within the following 2 years with the dramatic decline in the frequency of meetings of the Politburo, Orgburo and Secretariat. Arfon Rees has claimed that this marked a major shift in Stalin's own power, creating a personal dictatorship. Stalin had certainly accrued a vast amount of power and was now clearly a dictator in the Kremlin; but there were times when even he could be challenged by his 'loyal lieutenants', although these challenges were always kept within the boundaries of what was acceptable. J. Arch Getty's claim that a 'committee culture' governed Soviet high politics therefore deserves consideration. Getty accepts that there was a general move away from Politburo meetings and that Stalin was still the all-powerful leader, but he argues that this shift in power did not favour Stalin alone: the small group of 'oligarchs' who were Stalin's closest comrades also benefited. He argues that decisions were taken by leading figures meeting in 'quartets', 'sextets' and 'septets', informal ad hoc groups outside the Politburo, so that there was little reason for the Politburo to meet. Getty thus sees Soviet politics sharing a key characteristic with Western democracies, where important decisions are often made outside the meetings of cabinets and committees. For Getty, this meant that the Politburo had been 'normalised'.

Both Rees and Getty show how the party and its ruling bodies were gradually becoming marginalised within the system. Whether power lay in Stalin's hands alone or whether his most trustworthy comrades were allowed to share it is open to interpretation, but by the end of 1932 the system was clearly becoming more personalised and was definitely 'Stalinist'. An important element of this Stalinism was repression and murder, which visited the party and the country with a vengeance in the second half of the 1930s. The year 1932 was a turning point, as Nadya's suicide came at a time when Stalin and his closest comrades were enjoying life and it left him feeling less compassion than ever towards his fellows.

The secret lives of the Kremlin

Away from the high politics of anti-oppositionist struggles, life for those close to Stalin contrasted sharply with the harsh reality of peasant life on the collective farms or the hardships suffered by the industrial workers. For Stalin's closest 'loyal lieutenants' this was a time when the relationships between them had time to develop. They were mostly the men who had sided with him before and during the revolutionary era. Some shared his Georgian background; others simply shared his ruthless determination to make Soviet Russia a strong and powerful country. They had been promoted through the ranks of the Communist Party by Stalin and owed their political careers to him. These men, such as Grigory Ordzhonikidze, Kliment Voroshilov, Vyacheslav Molotov, Lazar Kaganovich and Lavrenty Beria, were as loyal to Stalin the man as they were to Stalin the leader: their loyalty during the early Bolshevik days earned them their later positions.

Like Stalin, Grigory Ordzhonikidze, known as Sergo, came from Georgia; this gave the young revolutionaries common ground on which to build a long-term friendship. Sergo sided with the Bolshevik faction of the RSDLP after he joined in 1903 and he was exiled for his underground revolutionary activities. He joined the Bolshevik Central Committee in 1912, the same year as Stalin, and was a key figure during the Civil War, working with Stalin to establish Soviet rule in Georgia. A member of Stalin's Politburo, from 1931 he was chairman of *Vesenkha* and then Commissar for Heavy Industry, thus playing a major role in the industrialisation of the country. Until his death in 1937, Ordzhonikidze was an important member of Stalin's so-called 'Caucasian clique'.

Kliment Voroshilov was a Ukrainian revolutionary who joined the Bolshevik Party in 1903, the same time as Ordzhonikidze and a year before Stalin. He joined Stalin's tight-knit group of southern Communists. This Stalinist clique was growing ever stronger and during the Civil War when Voroshilov was an army commander, he and Stalin formed an anti-Trotsky alliance in Tsaritsyn (later Stalingrad). Trotsky wrote that while here, Stalin 'shaped his intrigue against me with the aid of the…opposition of Voroshilov'. Voroshilov was elected to the Central Committee in 1921 and was People's Commissar for Defence between 1934 and 1940, only losing the post when it became clear that he was not capable of defending the USSR. After the death of the Commissar for War Mikhail Frunze in 1925, Voroshilov adopted Frunze's son. Caring for the children of fallen comrades was not uncommon among leading figures in the party: even Stalin's son Artyom was adopted. Voroshilov's friendship with Stalin saved him from the purges of the armed forces in the 1930s and he died in Moscow in 1969.

Lazar Kaganovich was one of Stalin's tougher henchmen. Like Voroshilov he was born in Ukraine but he only joined the Bolshevik Party in 1911, some years after his Ukrainian comrade. Kaganovich fought in the Civil War and declared Soviet power in Gomel in Belorussia; Stalin made him head of the organisational department (Orgburo) of the Central Committee in 1922. He was First Secretary of the Communist Party of Ukraine between 1925 and 1928 and he was elected to the Politburo in 1930. In the same year he became First Secretary of the Moscow City Communist Party and oversaw the construction of the impressive Moscow metro system. This was carried out at the expense of many of the city's cathedrals, including the Cathedral of Christ the Saviour, whose destruction acted as a forceful reminder of the Communists' atheism. Kaganovich showed the cruel side to his character during the Purges: as well as fulfilling his own purging 'duties', regardless of the suffering they caused, he failed to speak up for his own brother after he learned that Lavrenty Beria of the NKVD wanted to arrest him. His brother, also a high-ranking Communist minister, subsequently committed suicide. Kaganovich also cared little for his fellow Jews, who complained about his anti-Semitism. He remained a loyal Stalinist right up to his death in 1991.

Vyacheslav Molotov hailed from Kukarka in northeastern European Russia. He joined the Bolsheviks in 1905, a year after Stalin, and was first a loyal Leninist and then a loyal Stalinist. Together with Stalin he epitomised the victory of the bureaucracy over the idealists after Lenin's death. Molotov could be petty at times, correcting people if they got Lenin's nickname for him wrong (Lenin had called him 'iron arse' because of his unrelenting work rate, but some people mistakenly called him 'stone-arse' instead). He always supported Stalin over big issues, although he was not afraid to argue with his master. This took skill and diplomacy and may help to explain how he survived the Purges. He became People's Commissar for Foreign Affairs in 1939 and signed the Nazi–Soviet pact the same year. He outlived his boss and died in 1986, by which time he could be seen sitting on Moscow park benches and queuing up for food like everyone else.

The final 'loyal lieutenant' was the infamous Lavrenty Beria. If Stalin was like a mafia boss then Beria was his chief gangster. Like his master, Beria was a Georgian. He had been active in post-revolutionary politics, joining the Bolshevik Party in 1917 and the secret police in 1921, and it was in this period that he first met Stalin. Beria made contact with him again in the mid-1920s when he was Chairman of the OGPU in Georgia. Some accounts suggest that he cemented this relationship by giving Stalin information about the 'disloyal' behaviour of certain leading figures in the Georgian party. Although this helped Beria to become a close and trusted comrade of Stalin's, others saw him as unscrupulous and despicable. He pursued the collectivisation of Transcaucasia in a brutal fashion, headed the Transcaucasian secret police administration and in 1934 became a member of the party Central Committee. Stalin's family hated him and he was an unwelcome guest at the Stalin family dacha. Nadya told Stalin, 'That man must not be allowed to set foot in our house' and declared, 'He's a scoundrel!' Stalin replied that he was his friend and 'a good Chekist [secret policeman]'. Beria was a sycophant, praising Stalin endlessly and shamelessly. He replaced Nikolai Yezhov as head of the NKVD in 1938 and was universally feared, which ultimately proved his undoing after Stalin's death in 1953: his rivals in the Politburo, fearing that he would purge them, quickly had him arrested and executed. He was one of the true 'monsters' in Stalin's entourage who used his political position for his own personal, and even sexual, gratification.

One of the best accounts of how the Stalinist leaders lived and interacted with one another comes in Simon Sebag Montefiore's 2003 study *Stalin: The*

Court of the Red Tsar. As the title of this more personal, less political study suggests, Montefiore labels the Soviet leader a 'tsar' and suggests that Communist existence at the highest levels was similar to that of a royal court. However, the 'tsarism' that was evident within the Stalinist clique could at times give way to less hostile and more friendly acts of kindness. Nikita Khrushchev, who followed Stalin into power after the dictator's death in 1953, recalled how he was 'literally spellbound by Stalin, by his attentiveness, his concern...I was overwhelmed by his charm.' Stalin's daughter Svetlana remembered her early years with Stalin with affection, as her *papochka* (an affectionate version of 'papa') would kiss her and call her 'little sparrow'. She recalled that her father could be a loud, humorous family man who, together with her mother Nadya, created a friendly household at the Zubalovo dacha 20 miles outside Moscow (except, perhaps, when Beria was present). Zubalovo was one of the places Stalin used to relax and to entertain comrades, friends and relatives.

Svetlana recalled that the house was filled with children's voices and cheerful people who contributed to a happy atmosphere 'where my father was neither a god nor a "cult" but just the father of a family'. He enjoyed being around his comrades' children: Lazar Kaganovich's daughter Natasha would accompany him to the cinema. Those inside Stalin's inner circle enjoyed sharing their experiences of parenthood as they watched their comrades' children grow up. However, this picture of happy family life should be contrasted with the struggles faced by parents raising children in the countryside during collectivisation.

For the Stalinist leaders life in the Kremlin grounds or at their dachas was relaxing, friendly and intimate. Should comrades drop by to borrow something, Stalin would often invite them in for dinner. He could be a welcoming host, holding dinner parties which involved long drinking sessions. Tellingly, Stalin often kept himself out of these drinking bouts, thus ensuring that he remained in control, both of himself and of the situation. This is not to suggest that he was not a heavy drinker — he certainly could be — but rather it is a comment on his cunning: getting people drunk allowed him to extract information from them that they might not have been so willing to share when sober. The dinners, the drinking, the caring for fallen comrades' children all made the Kremlin a warm and friendly place for those lucky enough to be a part of Stalin's 'inner circle'. They formed intimate friendships, and Voroshilov's wife Yekaterina later wrote that it had been a 'wonderful time' with 'simple, nice, friendly relationships'.

Of course, Stalin could be the exact opposite of the kindly, welcoming 'Uncle Joe' character depicted here. Quite apart from his lack of compassion for those who suffered under collectivisation and industrialisation, he could also turn against those who were close to him. Svetlana noted, 'Years of friendship and fighting side by side in a common cause might as well never have been…he could wipe it all out at a stroke.' When Svetlana was a teenager, Stalin grew ever more irritated by her independent spirit and when she met and fell in love with a Jewish filmmaker the man was sent to a Siberian prison camp for 10 years, almost certainly on her father's orders.

Stalin's old comrade of the 1920s Nikolai Bukharin, whose fate was sealed when he disagreed with Stalin at the end of the decade, poignantly commented on this more cruel side of Stalin's nature. While in Paris Bukharin spoke with the Menshevik leader Fedor Dan and, learning that Dan knew little of Stalin, Bukharin explained that Stalin was 'unfortunate in not being able to convince everyone, including himself, that he is bigger than everyone', noting, 'If someone can speak better than he can, that person is doomed, as he won't let him remain alive, because that man is a constant reminder to him that he is not the first, not the very best.' Bukharin concluded with the chilling words that Stalin was a 'little, evil man, no, not a man, a devil'. These contrasting images of Stalin demonstrate that he could be a complex character, at times loving, kind and friendly and at others cold-hearted, vengeful and 'devil-like'. He proved to be many of these things while married to his second wife Nadya.

A troubled marriage

The union between Stalin and Nadya was always likely to be difficult, given Stalin's declaration that any warm feelings he had for people had died with his first wife. Nevertheless, Nadya penetrated Stalin's soul in a way that he clearly had not believed possible. They shared a loving if complicated marriage, as both were passionate, insecure people needing constant reassurance; if this was not forthcoming, insecurity, jealousy and misdirected anger followed. Those closest to Stalin knew that his relationship with Nadya could be stormy and that his wife would not simply accept a subservient role. She was called a 'peppery woman'; one comrade wondered how Stalin put up with the way Nadya was always 'nagging and humiliating' him. Hostile exchanges could even spill over into public outings; Simon Sebag Montefiore shows that Nadya was not afraid to fight back. The night of her suicide was the ultimate example of her resistance to Stalin's powerful will.

The fateful night, 8 November 1932, began with a party at Voroshilov's house to celebrate the fifteenth anniversary of the Bolshevik Revolution. Jealousy and anger accompanied Stalin and Nadya to the party; husband and wife both flirted with other guests at the party. Nadya's flirting may have been a result of Stalin's failure to notice that she was looking more glamorous than usual.

Communists and their partners were normally expected to adhere to a strict 'proletarian' dress code, but that night, excited about the party, Nadya had dressed more attractively. Stalin's lack of reaction wounded her.

Nadya had grown up in a Bolshevik family. She had been politically active from a young age and had been a typist for both Lenin and Stalin. She was also loyal to her husband and to many of his interpretations of the ideas of Marx and Lenin; however, by the early 1930s Nadya had begun to feel very troubled by the harshness of the collectivisation policy and its consequences. When Stalin proposed a toast to the destruction of the enemies of the people she did not join in. He angrily asked her why she was not drinking, even though he knew she disapproved of the starvation the peasantry were suffering under collectivisation. Making as much of a scene as he could, he threw things at her, calling out, 'Hey, you! Have a drink!' to which she replied, 'My name isn't "Hey"!' Nadya got up from the dinner table and stormed out of the room, telling her husband to 'shut up'. This evening was one of the rare occasions when Stalin drank heavily, which only made the situation worse: he clearly did not care how hurt his wife was and declared her a 'fool'.

Molotov's wife Polina went after Nadya to check on her and they walked around the Kremlin grounds. Nadya said that her husband often flirted with other women and was continually complaining. Polina calmed her down but also criticised her for adding to Stalin's stress at such a difficult political time. This was not necessarily what Nadya needed to hear, but she began to calm down and started to discuss her future in the party. When Polina felt sure Nadya was no longer upset she said goodnight and both women went home.

It is impossible to know exactly what happened next. Nadya did leave a letter but its specific contents are unknown, although Svetlana later said that Stalin was wounded and shocked by its contents. She also read, or at least had in her possession, a copy of Ryutin's 'platform'. It is difficult to determine the significance of this. The obvious implication is that Nadya had become so disenchanted with her husband's lack of compassion for those suffering in the countryside that she had decided to join the anti-Stalinist opposition. However, as she always remained loyal to her husband and to the party, it is perhaps more likely that she was simply reading Stalin's copy of the document and this may have fuelled her anger at this particular aspect of Stalinist policy, or it may be that, in the dark quiet of night, the suffering of the Soviet masses at the hands of her husband simply added to her own depression. With a small pistol in her hand she decided that she could no longer play a part in the world that Stalin was creating. She shot herself in the head.

Stalin had remained with his comrades, drinking into the night. When he finally came home he did not check to see how Nadya was after their argument;

instead he went to his own room (the two had separate rooms because of Stalin's late working hours). Had he looked in on Nadya he would have found her dead, lying in a pool of blood with a pistol by her side; as it was, the dreadful discovery was left to the housekeeper the following morning. Frantic discussions followed about what to do. The housekeeper called the nanny and they chose not to wake Stalin, probably because they did not want to be the ones to break the news to their powerful and paranoid boss. Instead they called other Communist leaders, including Voroshilov, Molotov and his wife. Nadya's brother Pavel and her parents Sergei and Olga were also informed.

This small group of devastated people had moved into the dining room to discuss what to do next when Stalin entered the room. The task fell to Stalin's old friend Yenukidze, who reportedly said: 'Josef, Nadezhda Sergeevna is no longer with us…Nadya is dead.' Immediately Stalin went into a deep state of shock: the 'man of steel' was once again broken by the loss of the woman he loved. He retreated to his room and stayed there grieving for days. He agonised over whether he had been a bad husband, telling Molotov that he had 'had no time to take her to the cinema'. He seemed more vulnerable than ever, declaring through his tears that 'she's crippled me' and that he and the children needed her so much. He asked why this had happened again and said he would resign and kill himself because he could not 'go on living like this'.

As it turned out, this statement had a certain truth: he and the children did indeed change their ways. Stalin returned to the more Spartan way of life of the Bolshevik revolutionary and the family moved out of the family apartment, swapping it for Bukharin's: Bukharin was glad to make this heartfelt gesture to help his old comrade, although his generosity would not help him later. Svetlana recalled that their 'carefree life, so full of gaiety and games…fell apart the moment my mother died'. Kaganovich noted that after 1932 'Stalin changed'. If we are to believe Stalin's nephew, Nadya's suicide forced the Soviet leader to take an even darker path than the one he was already on, making the blood-letting later in the decade 'inevitable'. Although this oversimplifies a complex issue, Nadya's suicide may well have made Stalin feel more detached when signing death warrants by the thousand or sending Bukharin to his fate.

Conclusion

The year 1932 was crucial in the development of Stalinism. It marked the point when Stalin gained more control over the party than ever, allowing him to make it his own party and his own system. Defeating the final challenges to his power left the road open for him to take absolute control and turn the Marxist ideal of 'dictatorship of the proletariat' into a far more personal dictatorship. The fact that this coincided with the shocking death of Nadya led Stalin to become more ruthless and more paranoid: he now saw threats and challenges everywhere. Both J. Arch Getty and Oleg V. Naumov (1999, p. 54) conclude that it is no exaggeration to say that the Ryutin platform 'began the process that would lead to terror': 1932 was the year when Stalin the tyrant was born, and this terrible child would quickly reach adulthood.

Questions

1 How might Soviet history have been different had Nadya Alliluyeva not killed herself?

2 What prevented the Oppositionists from launching a coup and toppling Stalin?

3 What are the advantages and disadvantages of using the imagery of a tsar to analyse Stalin?

Reference

- Getty, J. A., and Naumov, O. V. (1999) *The Road to Terror: Stalin and the Self-Destruction of the Bolsheviks, 1932–1939*, Yale University Press.

Chapter 5

Stalinist propaganda: was there any truth behind the lies?

As Stalinism developed, it created millions of disaffected people. Economic reconstruction through industrialisation and collectivisation wrought havoc in many areas of the country; at the same time Stalin's personal power was growing ever stronger, which doomed any political challenges from inside the party to failure. These aspects of the emerging Stalinist system paint a decidedly grim picture of life in Stalin's Soviet Union. However, Stalin's policies did bring improvements to the lives of many citizens, a fact which can be overlooked. There was genuine support for Stalin, coupled with a belief that a 'new civilisation' was being built, but a note of caution must be added here, as Soviet propaganda maintained similar, though far more exaggerated, claims.

This chapter challenges both the official view of life in the USSR, that socialism was successfully being constructed by happy workers and peasants, and the traditional assumption that life was terrible for everyone outside Stalin's ruling elite. It looks at some of the details of Stalin's Cultural Revolution and Stalinist propaganda and shows that the reality of Soviet life fell somewhere between the official images of happy workers and peasants striding confidently along the path to socialism and the 'totalitarian' view of the USSR. The official claims greatly embellished the experiences of many factory workers who may have broadly supported the aims and objectives of Stalin and the Communist Party; the totalitarian view ensured that the worst horrors of Stalinism were used to shape people's views of both the country and socialism itself.

Neither the contemporary propaganda nor the totalitarian idea allows for a serious exploration of the genuine support Stalin enjoyed or of evidence that life really did improve for many citizens when compared with the lives of their parents in pre-Revolutionary Russia. The Communist Party widened participation in education and promoted literacy campaigns, which had a profound effect on both the Soviet system and the lives of workers and peasants. It was hoped that this would help to create a 'New Soviet Person', although in reality it laid the basis for the emergence of a new kind of Soviet middle class. So there were clear improvements in the USSR, but this does not necessarily mean that socialism was being constructed. Moreover, as we shall see, because of the dark nature of Stalinism, those who did benefit from the system could not be certain that these improvements would last.

The Cultural Revolution and radicalism from below

Between 1928 and 1931, as part of the overhaul of the Soviet system, Stalin led a 'Cultural Revolution' which accompanied the 'Revolution From Above'. It coincided with the end of the NEP and the start of the economic restructuring of the Soviet Union. A policy of class discrimination led to radical proletarians attacking those 'bourgeois' elements that had re-emerged during the reintroduction of capitalism under the NEP. Stalin's Cultural Revolution sought to change how people viewed and understood everything, from art, literature and music to technical skills and work discipline. Its aim was to create an intelligentsia of proletarian origin, of 'Red Experts' who were both technologically able and ideologically sound and who could replace the old managers and so end the reliance on bourgeois specialists.

By creating a new political elite from the party's lower ranks, Stalin could command loyalty from those who were given these new positions. Newly qualified workers promoted by the Stalinist hierarchy were often more likely to respond positively to Moscow's orders than older Bolsheviks who might have opposed Stalin at an earlier juncture. It was also no coincidence that a trial of bourgeois specialists took place in 1928. The Shakhty show trial was put on after a number of specialists (*spetsy*) were charged with 'wrecking' and 'sabotage' in the Shakhty coalmines in Ukraine; Stalin used these supposed attacks on Soviet industry as an excuse to end the NEP and declare that proletarian experts were necessary.

This challenge to existing ideas saw a wave of radicalism and ideological militancy from young party workers who had become disenchanted with the lack of progress that the party had made in introducing socialism. These were the people who supported Stalin during the power struggle: the young urban proletariat who favoured the 'grand scheme' idea of rapid industrialisation. They responded by becoming aggressive to managers and the intelligentsia, which fostered a climate of suspicion, even loathing, of those who were perceived to be in privileged positions.

This response developed into significant pressure 'from below' on those in the higher echelons of the party. Workers and party activists who believed that the NEP had improved peasants' lives at their expense demanded that radical socialist policies be introduced to move the country away from capitalism and towards socialism. In some cases, workers and young party members from the Komsomol (Communist Union of Youth) became almost puritanical, opposed to drinking and smoking, which they saw as bourgeois pastimes. Such attitudes helped to create an extremist atmosphere and to undermine the moderation of the NEP period; much of the popular support for rapid industrialisation emerged during the late 1920s and early 1930s.

Going to the people

Belief in the Stalinist message saw thousands of urban party workers 'go to the people', which was a part of the revolutionary tradition in Russia dating back to the mid-nineteenth century. In the late 1920s and early 1930s Communist brigades, known as the 'twenty-five-thousanders', spread the Stalinist word in the villages. Groups of urban dwellers, mostly young people, militant workers and party officials, were sent out to persuade or coerce peasants to join the collective farms. These hastily trained workers, who spent 2 weeks on special courses to prepare for their mission, did not simply repeat the party's words without believing in what they were doing. One twenty-five-thousander, Lev Kopelev, recalled how Stalin's words had driven him on: 'Stalin said that the "struggle for bread is the struggle for socialism". I was convinced that we were the soldiers on an invisible front, waging war on kulak sabotage for the sake of bread that the country needed for the Five-Year Plan.'

Although Communists like Kopelev believed wholeheartedly in what they were doing, villagers who listened to him and his comrades often failed to accept their message with the same conviction. This was bound to be a problem when idealists from the city struggled to convince peasants about the benefits of the more modern farming techniques demanded by the party. We saw in Chapter 3 what happened when peasants resisted Moscow's will.

As Marxists, the Communist Party rejected belief in the existence of God, issuing widespread atheistic propaganda and launching an attack on the Orthodox Church. Literature espousing secular proletarian values was produced and this more radical assault on religion was reflected in the League of Militant Godless, originally founded in 1925 without the word 'Militant' in its title. Twenty-five-thousanders destroyed church bells and sent them off to industrial plants to be melted down for the Five-Year Plan, and churches were turned into 'museums of atheism'.

A climate of fear

Communist workers also denounced those in higher places, setting the country on course for the later purges. Denouncing the privileged fostered an environment in which egalitarian ideals were encouraged, although this changed quite quickly once workers who had denounced their bosses moved up in the world as a consequence. 'Cleansing' (or in Soviet terms 'purging') the party created a climate of fear for many enterprise managers and in 1930 the British ambassador in Moscow, Sir Esmond Ovey, wrote to the foreign secretary, Arthur Henderson, commenting that 51,000 state employees had already been purged from their posts and suggesting that one cause of this was the 'idealism of the members of the "chistkas" [purges]'.

Attacking and removing those who were perceived to be privileged or of a higher class, such as workers' managers, was a consequence of the Cultural Revolution's espousal of 'proletarian' values. Ovey showed considerable foresight when he wrote that such a practice 'may easily prove…to be…dangerous' and likely to 'lead to serious injustices' as this idealism 'may become subordinate to personal motives, and the temptation to turn a man out of his job in order to secure it for themselves must be a severe one'. Such acts were common during the much more extensive purge of the party between 1936 and 1938.

The posts of those who had been purged needed to be filled, and this process contributed to the emergence of a 'quicksand society': this saw a huge degree of 'downward mobility' hit bourgeois specialists and kulaks during collectivisation, but had a positive effect for workers who moved up into the bureaucracy, which offered the chance of a better life. These people were beneficiaries of Stalin's Cultural Revolution, which had created a system staffed by workers rather than by former owners and specialists. Originally from lower positions, these upwardly mobile workers (*vydvizhentsy*) were assigned to training for higher posts and became foremen, supervisors or specialists themselves. There was, of course, a danger that those who rose to the top as a result of the denunciation of others could lose their jobs in the same manner. Thus Stalinism created a society in a constant state of flux.

Those who were pulled up into the administrative side of the system or into better industrial jobs were often initially unqualified for their new roles, and this meant that there was a great need for more educational opportunities across the USSR. When the first Five-Year Plan uncovered shortages of qualified personnel the party's response was to ensure that more people received education. Extending opportunities for secondary or higher education had been a part of the Bolshevik programme since the revolution and had successfully improved literacy rates across the country. Lenin decreed that illiteracy was to be eradicated, demanding that children and adults must be literate in their own language. This campaign to 'liquidate illiteracy' (*likbez*) was very successful and continued during the Cultural Revolution. Literacy rates rose from around 40% to nearly 90% in 20 years.

Propaganda and the Cult of Stalin

By greatly increasing the numbers of people who could read, the Communist Party ensured that there was a wider audience for its written propaganda. The Stalinist system relied heavily on this political tool as a means of maintaining its power, and its portrayal of a country at peace with itself while building a new society gave the Communist Party an air of legitimacy. A fundamental part of Stalinist propaganda was the virtual deification of Stalin through the cult of personality, also known as the Cult of Stalin. This shared obvious characteristics with the Cult of Lenin created by Stalin almost immediately after Lenin's death and, as we shall see, it had a number of purposes, including linking Stalin to the country's achievements and portraying him as Lenin's heir. This personalisation of power coincided with the process by which the dictatorship of the proletariat became the dictatorship of Stalin.

The party used propaganda to help consolidate its gains from the first Five-Year Plan and to widen the image of the New Soviet Person at work and rest. Campaigns were instigated to inspire people to work harder and awards were given out, such as the 'Hero of Labour', most evident during Stakhanovism. Newsreels and films showed a happy, enthusiastic population of builders of socialism in the factories and fields. Poetry, songs, art and literature were now all governed by 'Socialist Realism', which pushed the party line through the creative arts.

The building of stadiums, parks and palaces of culture was used as a means of inspiring people to believe that a new civilisation was dawning. Stalin's speeches reminded the population: 'Life has improved, comrades, life has become more joyous', and this message was hung on a banner across the gates of Gorky Park in Moscow. Grand statues were put up celebrating the link between worker and peasant, often showing a male worker holding a hammer aloft next to a female collective farmer holding a sickle. Statues of Lenin and

Stalin sprang up in cities and villages across the country and acted as an ever-present reminder of Stalin's supposed power; the party actively promoted the idea that Stalin knew everything that was happening throughout the Soviet Union.

Party propaganda extended further than simply erecting statues, hanging banners from public buildings and holding rallies. The rapid expansion of education allowed the party to teach Soviet citizens its particular syllabus, which included compulsory lessons in Marxism-Leninism to ensure that the population was well-versed in the state's ideology. The party also imposed officially approved textbooks in schools. The authority of teachers was restored as they were given back the power to award marks for tests and exams, which in some areas after the revolution had been given to students. This more conservative mood also saw the return to pre-Revolutionary norms such as the wearing of school uniforms and the reintroduction of fees for the upper forms of secondary schools, which prepared children for higher education. History classes were taught about the 'reforming' tsars, Ivan IV ('Ivan the Terrible') and Peter the Great, as they were examples of how Russia could be modernised, albeit through brutal means. This latter policy also reflected the needs of the Stalin cult.

In the wider society, propaganda and culture intertwined to give the New Soviet Person a specifically Stalinist cultural background. Stakhanovites were expected not only to be Heroes of Labour but also to be educated in the ways of the party and in Russian culture. To better themselves, workers were to improve their reading skills if these were weak and to encourage their wives to enjoy the theatre or concerts. Workers who had read the *History of the Communist Party of the Soviet Union (Bolsheviks): short course*, as well as Russian classics such as *War and Peace*, were praised as successful products of the system.

The public and private worship of the party, of communism and of Stalin were fundamentally important elements of the propaganda campaigns. Citizens were encouraged to have a 'Lenin corner' in their workplaces and homes, where a picture of the USSR's founder was placed on a table or a wall, together with other Leninist and Communist objects. Stalin's picture was also to be found everywhere, often accompanying Lenin's as a reminder that Stalin was supposedly Lenin's closest comrade. Plaques were made in pairs, one with Stalin's face and one with Lenin's, while handmade silk flags showing Stalin and Lenin had inspiring words sewn onto them, such as 'Under the banner of Lenin, under the leadership of Stalin, forward we go to the victory of communism.'

Part of this Cult of Stalin meant that 'good Stalinists' had to repeat the party line whenever in conversation, to such an extent that when the British trade union leader Walter Citrine visited the USSR he found that 'scarcely a speech is made without eulogistic references to "our beloved leader, Comrade Stalin"'. He said that everyone had to ask himself, '"What is the true Leninist line? What would Stalin say?"…To argue with a Russian communist is to argue with a gramophone record of Stalin.' Thinking 'like Stalin' and displaying his picture in numerous places reflected this most personalised aspect of Soviet propaganda.

The General Secretary's rise to god-like status began in 1929, when the title *vozhd'* was used at his fiftieth birthday celebrations and *Pravda* printed numerous congratulatory messages. This was the start of a cult of personality that grew to outlandish proportions, with even some of his defeated opponents from the power struggle being called on to praise Stalin. Bukharin called him the 'field marshal of the proletarian forces', while Kamenev declared that this was 'the era of Stalin'. This personalisation of power effectively linked Stalin to all the country's successes while giving the 'wise leader' the power to denounce any other individual when things went wrong: after all, it couldn't possibly be Stalin's fault.

Stalin was the personification of the party's 'benevolent' rule and its role in building a new civilisation. Posters showed a smiling Stalin cuddling children, who were encouraged to love him more than their own parents. 'Reforming' tsars such as Ivan IV and Peter the Great were turned into national heroes and were used as examples of how strong and determined (i.e. oppressive) policies were necessary in the struggle to modernise the country. The use of Russian 'heroes' from the past also highlights how Russian culture was becoming more conservative and nationalistic.

A culture developed that encouraged excessive praise for all the main party leaders, with even cities being renamed in their honour — Tsaritsyn became Stalingrad, Vladikavkaz became Ordzhonikidze, Perm became Molotov — but Stalin was still praised more highly than everyone else. Stalin was portrayed as the only person capable of continuing Lenin's work; Stalin was presented as Lenin's most loyal disciple and photographs were doctored to show how close the two were; Stalin was worshipped in poems which claimed that it was he who 'brought man to birth', he 'who fructifies the earth', he 'who makes bloom the spring'.

The quasi-religious terms that were used to celebrate the 'genius' that was Stalin to some extent tapped into the centuries-old Russian Orthodox Christianity, which had been the official religion of the country and had shaped the ideas of many, including, of course, the young Stalin. The Soviet Union replaced God with Marx and Jesus with Lenin. Stalin was manoeuvred into a position akin to that of Jesus' closest disciple, John, while Trotsky became Judas or the Devil. Of course, this message was couched in terms of the class war rather than Russian Orthodoxy, but the point was the same: unite to defeat the enemy and Heaven awaits.

How far did the official image of Soviet life reflect the realities of the Soviet people? We know from our assessment of the lives of the peasants and workers during collectivisation and industrialisation that millions suffered greatly at the hands of the Stalinist state. However, according to Christopher Read (2001, pp. 109–110), Soviet propaganda presented a picture that was 'not so much out-and-out lies as a concoction of half truths' which had 'some grains of truth' in them. While remembering the horrors that Stalinism brought to many, it must also be acknowledged that some people did benefit from the system, as many thousands of workers and Communists were pulled up into the system, creating 'a huge cohort of beneficiaries from the cultural revolution' (Sandle 1999, p. 243). But who were these beneficiaries of Stalin's rule?

The positive impact of the Cultural Revolution

The opportunities for education that were opened up by the Cultural Revolution reached even greater levels from the late 1920s onwards and many more skilled workers entered the workplace. However, the need for these workers was so desperate that they often became only semi-skilled or semi-literate, which caused serious problems when using new machinery, as was shown in the Shakhty Affair (see Chapter 3). Nevertheless, thousands gained valuable education in colleges and universities and achieved levels of learning that their parents could never have dreamt of. The workers' faculty (*rabfak*) offered courses to those continuing their education. Viktor Kravchenko recalled that his family was very happy when he was selected for technical training: his father proudly told people, 'My son will be an engineer.'

The literacy campaign and growth of education rights created a population who could read and be influenced by Communist literature and propaganda. Examples of this included the official *History of the Communist Party of the Soviet Union (Bolsheviks): short course*, published in 1938. All pupils, students and teachers had to read this Stalinist, and therefore distorted, version of the Bolshevik revolution and the 'heroic' construction of socialism that followed, in which Lenin was portrayed as the great leader and Stalin as his only true disciple. This oversimplified version of events was easy for those with limited education and understanding of the party's background to understand. However, a long-term consequence of making education more accessible was the creation of a class of well-educated people whose heightened expectations became increasingly incompatible with the restrictive and repressive Stalinist system.

The emphasis on expanding education saw the number of school pupils increase from 14 million in 1929 to more than 20 million in 1931, with over 1 million university graduates by 1939. By 1933, more than 200,000 Communists had entered full-time education and around 1,500,000 were promoted into responsible administrative and specialist positions. There were more jobs than ever now available in the bloated bureaucracy, an essential feature of Stalinism since rapid industrialisation needed a vast administration to manage it.

Workers and working-class Communists benefited directly from Stalin's Cultural Revolution and many graduates from technical institutes experienced rapid promotion. Their good fortune was due to openings created either by the industrial advance or by the Purges. Many opportunities for 'upward mobility' were presented to people. Nadezhda Mandelstam, wife of the Soviet poet Osip Mandelstam, noted that everyone could hope that they would advance quickly, as every day somebody was removed from their job and needed to be replaced, a grim reminder that those who benefited from Stalinism often did so only at the expense of other, less fortunate individuals. However, what was important for Stalin was that the radical turnover of elite personnel created a large group of workers who were loyal to him and his system.

Upwardly mobile workers rose to high positions in three closely intercon-nected areas: industrial administration, the government and the party. Those in the final category often played a key role in the future leadership. Nikita Khrushchev (party leader after Stalin's death), Leonid Brezhnev (who replaced Khrushchev in this role) and Aleksei Kosygin (Brezhnev's prime minister) were all *vydvizhentsy*. People from middle-class backgrounds, with education in the humanities or law, were replaced in the party hierarchy by members from a working-class or peasant background, who had mainly enjoyed a technological education. This contributed to a growing legitimisation of the system, as this new elite saw themselves as self-made men, indebted to Stalin for their rapid rise to an improved life.

It was not only administrative workers who gained from Stalinism: workers were rewarded for breaking records in production. One worker who succeeded in this task was Aleksei Stakhanov, whose monumental efforts epitomised the campaign for overfulfilment of production plans. In 1935, Stakhanov, a coalminer in the Donbass region of Ukraine, cut 102 tonnes of coal in a single shift: the usual allotted amount was 7 tonnes. The party was anxious to utilise this feat to inspire other workers to achieve similar levels of production; the

Stakhanovite movement emerged as an attempt to recreate the popular radicalism and support for the regime that had existed at the height of the Cultural Revolution.

Stakhanovism spread to other industries and similar successes took place elsewhere. These were taken as evidence of the greatness of socialism and of Soviet socialist workers. Stakhanovism became a byword for breaking normal rates and Stakhanovites entered the Soviet elite, becoming the cream of the new Soviet 'aristocracy' (*znat'*). They received huge pay rises and the best of the new apartments that were being built for workers. However, this made them unpopular with their workmates, who were told they had to work harder to achieve similar levels. As hostility to Stakhanovites grew the movement ended, but it had shown that wealth could be redistributed towards workers who remained outside the bureaucracy.

Although some workers were joining the system's elite, the administrative and official stratum remained at the top while the working class and peasantry remained at the bottom. As this bureaucracy did everything it could to preserve its position, Stalinism became more concerned with maintaining the new hierarchy and privileges that came with it. Better-off workers and peasants occupied a position similar to that of the Western middle classes and a type of 'red' bourgeoisie emerged which enjoyed a better standard of living than other workers. It benefited from the *nomenklatura* system (a list system of appoint-ments within the party and other key areas), which could lead to lucrative promotions; the *nomenklatura* became an entire network within the Stalinist system. Those lucky enough to be included could gain access to special shops with better food than that usually on sale or to consumer goods at cheaper prices. More spacious apartments, special healthcare, subsidised holidays and better pay were also on offer. Stalinism could be a contradictory system, rewarding people by helping them to escape from the awful conditions that it had itself created and which so many others had to accept. These rewards, of course, were not necessarily permanent. Extra benefits could be removed as quickly as they were received: they were not owned by the recipient, since access to them came with the position.

As beneficiaries of Stalinism sought to hold on to what they had, they often became more conservative in their outlook. By the 1930s this helped to foster a more widespread conservatism that fed into the state's conventional outlook. Managers grew more concerned with enjoying a 'petit bourgeois' existence with a 'nice' house and 'lace curtains and pot plants' (quoted in Read 2001, p. 113); ideology became less important to party workers as they climbed a new social ladder. Although the party continued to make use of radical slogans in its attempt to build a new society, declaring that there were 'no fortresses the

Bolsheviks could not storm', it became more traditional in its actual policies, reintroducing school uniforms, enhancing the authority of the teacher, making divorce more difficult to obtain and launching campaigns to restore parental authority within strong family units. These became Stalinist norms and were used to promote social order.

Stalinism benefited those who were raised into the bureaucracy or the new Soviet elite, giving them material goods, access to special shops and new apartments, and better healthcare. These privileges were denied to many Soviet citizens, and even those lucky enough to be a part of the new elite could not be certain that their good fortune would last. There was no private ownership in the USSR: the state owned everything, which meant that the better homes and jobs and the luxuries that sometimes went with them could be removed as quickly as they were given out. So, of course, could the people who enjoyed them.

Conclusion

Stalinist society in the 1930s was in a constant state of flux. It was a 'quicksand society' where little stayed the same for long. What emerged from this upheaval was a contradictory system, born out of radicalism but becoming more conservative as it stabilised during the early 1930s. It is therefore difficult to conclude that a socialist system was created; instead, Stalinism grew more concerned with privilege and hierarchy than with fair redistribution of wealth and egalitarian socialism. Although Stalin was concerned to make Russia a more modern country, Stalinism did, in some ways, revert to the old tsarist order, where the working and peasant classes obeyed their masters. This created a divided society, with a 'them and us' mentality.

The main difference was that the masters (or 'them') were supposed to be on the side of the workers ('us'), representing their interests and acting as a 'vanguard' that would create a socialist state. Soviet propaganda sought to convince people that Stalin was their friend, that the party was the benevolent force in a rapidly changing world and that a 'New Soviet Person' was being born. The realities witnessed and experienced by Soviet citizens, however, were often very different.

Nevertheless, there were those whose lives did improve, either temporarily or for the long term. Certain policies helped to lift workers out of their lowly positions and gave them a chance of a better standard of living than they or their parents had had. These workers had a valuable role to play, as 'their input, their goals, their aspirations…profoundly influenced the evolution of the system'; this view of less passive social groups goes against the traditional 'totalitarian' view of Soviet history (Hosking 1992, pp. 205–06). However, the ways in which certain people's lives improved shows the contradictory nature of Stalinism: many of these *vydvizhentsy* who benefited from Stalin's rule did so at the expense of others who lost their jobs, their freedom and even their lives in the great upheaval. The 'new civilisation', as the British socialists Sidney and Beatrice Webb called Soviet communism in the mid-1930s, was far removed from the Bolshevik promises of 1917 and, for many people, it failed to live up to the images of a happy and equal society portrayed in Stalinist propaganda.

Questions

1 How wise was it for Stalin to rely so heavily on the young?

2 How fair is it to compare the Cult of Stalin with those of Hitler or Mussolini? In what ways were the cults different?

3 How was it possible to flourish under Stalin's regime?

References

- Hosking, G. (1992) *A History of the Soviet Union 1917–1991*, Fontana.
- Read, C. (2001) *The Making and Breaking of the Soviet System*, Palgrave.
- Sandle, M. (1999) *A Short History of Soviet Socialism*, Routledge.

Chapter 6

The Great Terror: how widespread was it?

In 1936 the Communist Party turned in on itself and the 'self-destruction of the Old Bolsheviks' took a sinister turn. Chapter 4 showed that Stalin dealt with opposition within the party by expelling comrades from their positions. Much to his annoyance, other Politburo members stopped him imposing the death sentence; however, he only had to wait a few years until critics of his policies were executed by the NKVD. With one eye on the recent past, when he had defeated the Ryutin platform, Stalin relaunched the offensive against real or imagined opponents in the party. In September 1936, in a subtle reference to Ryutin, he declared that the secret police were '4 years behind' in their task of 'unmasking enemies'.

Between 1936 and 1938 a widespread purge (*chistka*) of undesirable elements took hold of the Communist Party, and it was 'cleansed' of supposedly questionable groups who, it was alleged, had been involved in anti-Soviet activities. Spurious allegations were made and many Old Bolsheviks (those comrades who had joined the party before the October Revolution) were found guilty of implausible charges during public show trials and sentenced to death. After the murder of the popular Communist leader Sergei Kirov (discussed below) the system thrived on mistrust and suspicion, which made it likely that the NKVD would extend its search for enemies to other areas of the system. The Red Army, enterprise managers, even the NKVD itself, were among groups that were attacked during the Purges, making this process different from previous 'cleansings'. It became an assault on the system as a whole, not simply on the party. Finally it reached further into the rest of society and became known as the 'Great Terror' (1937–38).

The Purges and wider terror have traditionally been seen as a conscious, deliberate attempt by Stalin to ensure that he had total control over the party and the population. All opposition was ruthlessly crushed and Old Bolsheviks who might have remembered the past differently from Stalin, and thus contradicted the official image of the *vozhd'*, were particularly at risk. The blame for the Purges has therefore been laid firmly at the feet of Stalin, the seemingly omnipotent Soviet leader.

A less personalised version of events does not remove this blame from Stalin, but shares his responsibility with institutional factors such as the NKVD, which had to ensure that it fulfilled its targets. This interpretation also demonstrates how the Purges provoked a cynical and panicky response from regional leaders and Soviet citizens as they reached further out into the country during the *Yezhovshchina* ('the time of *Yezhov*', the head of the NKVD). Some local party leaders used the upheaval to settle old scores with local enemies while other people denounced neighbours before they could be denounced themselves. Change thus came from above, via the public show trials and Moscow's orders to the regions, and from below as chaos and confusion reigned at local level.

Naturally, Stalin approved of what was happening, as he was paranoid in his belief that he had enemies everywhere and that they were being guided by the sinister hand of *Trotsky*. By publicly purging these 'opponents' he could send a message that opposition to his policies or to him personally would result in arrest followed by imprisonment or death. The two questions that concern us in looking at this most sinister aspect of the Stalinist system are: (a) what happened in this era of terror-fuelled change and (b) how widespread were its effects?

The death of Comrade Kirov

In January 1934, the Communist Party held its Seventeenth Congress, known as the 'Congress of Victors' as it celebrated the successes of industrialisation and collectivisation. The country was apparently well on the road to communism and the party took time out to acknowledge this great leap forward. Yet Stalin found that there was still dissent in the Communist ranks which, he believed, threatened his position in the Kremlin. Sergei Kirov was the Secretary of the Leningrad party. He was a loyal Stalinist, close to Stalin personally, and a popular member of the Communist Party. However, he and Stalin differed in their approaches to the agricultural sector after the initial collectivisation programme: Kirov wanted the party to take a more cautious line, with less exploitation of the peasants and a relaxation of its more coercive policies. This does not mean that he was in favour of a total change of direction, but rather that he hoped that less hostile policies would help bring stability to the country after the turmoil of the recent years.

Many delegates at the Seventeenth Congress agreed with Kirov. In a move that suggested a growing desire to get Kirov to Moscow, some 300 delegates voted against Stalin when Congress voted for the new Central Committee, while Kirov received massive support, with only a handful of negative votes. This sent a clear message to Stalin that many party members were unhappy with the excessive suffering that had accompanied collectivisation. Kirov's star was rising and he seemed destined for great things.

However, late on a winter's afternoon on 1 December 1934, Leonid Nikolaev walked into the Smolny Institute, where the Leningrad party had its headquarters, and shot Kirov dead. He then turned his gun on himself but was stopped from committing suicide by a passing electrician. Nikolaev was forced to answer for his crime, but he might not have expected to be questioned about the assassination by the most powerful man in the USSR. Stalin travelled to Leningrad the day after the murder of his close friend: he wanted to oversee the police operation personally. This was an unusual decision: the NKVD was a powerful organisation and should have been able to deal with the situation. When Stalin reached Leningrad he reprimanded the local NKVD for its failure, angrily striking its Leningrad commander, Filip Medved. After visiting the hospital where Kirov's body lay, Stalin set up his own investigation in his dead friend's office in the Smolny. He brought with him a number of close colleagues, including Vyacheslav Molotov, Deputy Procurator Andrei Vyshinsky, who became Prosecutor General during the Purges, and the head of the Central Committee's Personnel Department, Nikolai Yezhov.

Documents from the recently opened Soviet archives in Russia indicate that Nikolaev acted independently, shooting Kirov because he believed that Kirov was having an affair with his wife. Other reports have highlighted the alleged complicity of either Stalin or the NKVD in the murder. The way in which Stalin conducted his investigation suggests that he did not order Kirov's death and there is no evidence that conclusively proves his involvement. Indeed, soon after the murder, Stalin told his brother-in-law, Pavel Alliluyev, who was comforting the bereaved leader, that he was 'absolutely an orphan', probably a reference to his loss within 2 years of both his wife and his close friend. This does not mean, however, that Stalin did not use Kirov's death to strengthen his own position and the role of the NKVD. Stalin ignored the lack of evidence to suggest that Kirov's murder had been part of an organised terrorist plot by former comrades; suggesting that such a network of anti-Soviet terrorists existed reinforced the idea that powerful enemies of Stalin and the party were everywhere.

When Nikolaev was summoned to Stalin's presence, he seemed dazed and confused and did not recognise the General Secretary; it took a photograph of Stalin to make him believe that the *vozhd'* stood before him. It is difficult to be certain of exactly what happened during the meeting: accounts range from

Nikolaev showing remorse to his claiming that he was obeying party orders. Whatever the reason for Nikolaev's action, it was the start of the process that led to the Purges that took place between 1936 and 1938.

Tightening the law

On the day that Kirov was murdered, a decree was passed by the Politburo ushering in new anti-terrorist laws that gave more freedom to prosecutors. They no longer had to contend with defence lawyers and they could question suspects without having to rely on witnesses. The decree stated that the investigative agencies were to act with more urgency in cases of suspected acts of terror and that the judiciary was not to delay the execution of those found guilty: there was to be no chance of appeal. These were dangerous policies to enact at any time, but to pursue such a radical overhaul of the Soviet criminal code in a climate of fear and suspicion could only add to the insecurity that had been emerging since the late 1920s. Such a repressive decree was no surprise given that Genrikh Yagoda had been appointed as the first People's Commissar for Internal Affairs only a few months earlier. Yagoda was a loyal Stalinist and a fearsome individual who supervised the bloodletting during the early stages of the purges.

From December 1934, both Stalin and the NKVD became stronger in their respective positions and each fed off the other's insecurities and fears. This led to widespread repression in Leningrad and to a clampdown on any other alleged anti-Soviet activities. Leonid Nikolaev was tried at the end of December and the decree sanctioned at the start of the month ensured only one fate for him: he was shot within an hour of his sentence being passed.

In this cold winter month of December 1934 a further 6,501 people were shot. January 1935 saw two of Stalin's old comrades-turned-opponents, Zinoviev and Kamenev, arrested and blamed for Kirov's death. It was alleged that they had conspired with 17 others in an illegal organisation, the so-called 'Moscow centre', to carry out terrorist acts. They accepted responsibility for encouraging opposition but they denied any involvement in the death of Kirov. Kamenev claimed that he must have been blind as he had 'reached the age of 50 but have never seen this "centre" of which it appears I have been a member'. However, their acceptance that they had an 'oppositionist' past played into the hands of the Stalinist authorities, who could now make political capital out of it.

Zinoviev was sentenced to 10 years in prison, Kamenev to 5 years, with the rest of this supposed 'gang' of anti-Soviet agents being given varying jail sentences. There were other repressive consequences of the growing suspicion and tension. In 1935 a new law was introduced that stated that 'enemies of the

Motherland' were automatically guilty, that adult relations of anyone fleeing abroad would be exiled for 5 years, and that children over the age of 12 could be prosecuted and given the death penalty. Censorship was tightened: the works of Zinoviev, Kamenev and Trotsky, their supposed 'master', were removed from libraries and a society for Old Bolsheviks was shut down. Within 3 years of Kirov's death and the passing of the new decree, up to 2 million people had been sentenced to death or the gulag.

Some historians have claimed that the decree of 1 December 1934 became a charter of terror. The suggestion is that the timing of the decree is evidence that the purges were pre-planned and that Kirov was murdered on Stalin's orders both to remove a dangerous rival and to ensure total control over a compliant people through mass repression. However, it may be that the notoriously paranoid Stalin was shaken by the murder of his close friend and protégé and really did believe that there were enemies everywhere, so powerful that they could gain access to any government building and murder high-ranking officials: this would make the decree a panicky response by a nervous leader with no predetermined plot. The fact that Kirov's murder occurred at a time of increased tension, as internal and external threats to the stability of the country appeared to be growing, adds weight to this argument. While Stalin certainly seized this opportunity to tighten his grip on power, it is unlikely that he had anything to do with the actual murder of Kirov.

There may be some truth, however, in the claim that the NKVD was responsible for Kirov's death. Just as workers and peasants had plans to work to and quotas to fulfil, so Stalin's secret police had to ensure that they did not make themselves seem politically suspect by not completing their quotas. But what if there were not enough real spies or political opponents to constitute a danger to Stalin and the Soviet Union? The NKVD would have had to invent enemies to ensure their own reason to exist. According to this view, Stalin may not have been guilty of the murder but his secret police were.

The NKVD played upon the concerns that people had about the 'Trotskyites' and 'wreckers' to whom Stalin and the party propaganda machine constantly referred. One shocking anti-Soviet act, such as the murder of a popular party member, would be enough to secure the NKVD's own place at the Stalinist table, as Stalin would need a strong secret police to keep him and the USSR safe from enemies at home and abroad. Although the Kirov affair had petered out by the middle of 1935, it was only a matter of time before a new round of purges began.

Purging the party: the show trials

Purges had taken place in Lenin's time. He had felt it necessary to 'cleanse' the Bolshevik Party after the Civil War, as some of the best socialists had died fighting for the revolutionary cause and Lenin feared that their replacements were too careerist, out for personal gain rather than for the good of the party, the country or revolutionary socialism. The first purge took place in 1921 after the Tenth Party Congress, when the NEP and the ban on factions were introduced. During Lenin's purges people lost their party membership and, in extreme cases, where it was believed that they posed a counter-revolutionary threat, they were exiled.

Likewise, the use of show trials to remove political enemies was not invented by Stalin; Lenin had made an example of members of another left-wing party, the Socialist Revolutionaries, in 1922. Stalin however, focused more specifically on people from his own party, in some cases comrades who had been members for decades. A key difference between the purges under Lenin and Stalin was that opponents were allowed to live after Lenin's *chistka*, whereas Stalin's purges of 1936–38 led to death. Before a trial took place it was necessary to ensure that the accused would plead guilty; there was little point in putting on a show trial if it did not deter others from following the accused's alleged path. Confessions were obtained through torture and long police interrogations at the NKVD's Lubyanka headquarters in Moscow. Sleep deprivation was also a police tactic, as was threatening the families of the accused. Zinoviev and Kamenev, although subjected to intense interrogation, accepted their fate after Stalin promised that they would not suffer the death penalty. He lied.

In June 1936 Stalin ordered the NKVD to organise a trial of Trotskyists and Zinovievists and the Central Committee sent a secret letter to regional party bosses regarding 'terrorist activities' of the 'Trotskyist-Zinovievist counter-revolutionary bloc'. This led to the first show trial on 19 August 1936, where State Prosecutor Andrei Vyshinsky played a leading role in the annihilation of the Old Bolsheviks. One of his trademarks was the phrases he used to denounce those on trial. He demanded that the 'mad dogs', presumably Zinoviev and Kamenev, be shot, declared that Bukharin was 'the acme of monstrous hypocrisy…and inhuman villainy' and that Yagoda was 'surrounded, as with flies, with German, Japanese and Polish spies'. Vyshinsky's versatile vocabulary made a fair trial difficult, but this process, of course, was not about fairness.

Two of the accused at this first trial, Zinoviev and Kamenev, were Stalin's allies in the anti-Trotsky triumvirate of the 1920s power struggle; now they were thrown into the lion's den along with 14 other party officials. Ridiculous charges were made against supposed members of a 'Trotskyist-Zinovievist Centre'. The accused allegedly organised a clandestine terrorist centre, took their orders from Trotsky, murdered Kirov and plotted to do the same to other party leaders, including Stalin. The confessions signed by those on trial led many people at the time to believe the charges. Zinoviev stated that he was 'utterly guilty' of organising a group whose purpose was to kill Stalin, and that he was 'second only to Trotsky'. He pleaded guilty to the charge of organising Kirov's murder and of ignoring the party's warnings not to enter into an alliance with Trotsky. Likewise, Kamenev declared that he had 'guided this conspiracy' because he was a member of an oppositionist bloc that was unhappy at Stalin's success. He claimed that members of this group wanted to overthrow Stalin and acted in this way out of 'boundless hatred' and a 'lust for power'. All of the accused who took part in the first show trial were sentenced to death and shot on 24 August, including Kamenev and Zinoviev, who had been promised by Stalin that their lives would be spared. Some reports claim that Zinoviev pleaded for his life while Kamenev refused to degrade himself in this way; others, however, stated that both men grovelled on the floor, weeping.

The confessions of the accused also implicated other Old Bolsheviks, such as the former trade union leader Mikhail Tomsky. Vyshinsky declared that these figures would also be investigated. Tomsky committed suicide before he could be arrested but this did not stop the authorities from conducting a second trial, in January 1937, where another group of old revolutionaries was paraded in front of the Soviet press. Karl Radek, Yury Pyatakov and Grigory Sokolnikov were all denounced as members of the 'Anti-Soviet Trotskyite Centre'. They were accused of plotting the forcible overthrow of the Soviet government with help from Nazi Germany and Japan, of planning to restore capitalism in Russia and of working to sabotage and wreck Soviet industries.

This trial was similar to the earlier one in that both were arranged to remind Soviet citizens that Trotsky was the mastermind behind all actions against the Soviet Union, and that they should therefore be vigilant in the war against Trotskyism. All those who stood trial in January 1937 confessed to their 'crimes' and were found guilty. Pyatakov was sentenced to death by shooting, while Sokolnikov and Radek were given 10 years' imprisonment. Sokolnikov was murdered in prison by his cellmates, while Radek died 2 years later in a prison camp where, according to some reports, he was executed. A month after this second trial took place, Stalin's close friend and comrade Sergo Ordzhonikidze died suddenly. He had tried to restrain the excesses of the Stalinist purges and even protected some party members from the NKVD. Comrades later declared that he had been unhappy for some time, and that he committed suicide in

1937 after his brother was tortured and shot. 'Officially' Ordzhonikidze died of a heart attack.

The show trials were supposed to be about eliminating threats to the Soviet Union. However, the fact that two of Lenin's oldest comrades, Radek and Pyatakov, were tried adds weight to the argument that Stalin was deliberately removing long-standing members of the party who might have had alternative memories of defining moments in its history. Zinoviev and Kamenev had already been removed and now other Old Bolsheviks suffered a similar fate. Stalin was attacking the very basis of the old party network, although those who had been a part of *his* group before the revolution were generally safe. Trying Radek and Pyatakov also made the crimes appear more shocking at the time and the threat from 'anti-Soviet agents' even greater: if Lenin's old friends were now enemies of the state, who else might be?

The answer to this question came in the final trial, in March 1938, of 21 members of the 'Anti-Soviet Bloc of Rights and Trotskyists', including Nikolai Bukharin, Aleksei Rykov and Genrikh Yagoda. Yagoda's inclusion is perhaps most surprising, as only a few years earlier he had been the head of the NKVD, leading the search for 'wreckers' and 'Trotskyists'. This was the clearest evidence that nobody was safe from the Stalinist purges. The usual long list of crimes now included wrecking; undermining the Red Army; aiding foreign intelligence services to prepare an attack against the USSR; working for the end of socialism and the restoration of capitalism in Russia; the assassination of Kirov; and conspiring with Rightists, Trotskyists, Zinovievites and Mensheviks, to name but a few of the 'devilish' organisations trying to bring down the Soviet government. Confessions were secured from all those who stood trial, although Bukharin bravely pleaded not guilty to the counts of espionage and assassination. In his closing remarks Bukharin, while admitting the case against him, 'proceeded, uninterrupted…to tear it to bits, while Vyshinsky, powerless to intervene, sat uneasily in his place, looking embarrassed'. As usual, all the accused were found guilty and executed. Bukharin continued his defiance even when faced with death: one former Communist claimed that 'Bukharin and Rykov died with curses against Stalin on their lips. And they died standing up.'

In the end the party turned in on itself as the NKVD demanded ever more confessions to fulfil its quota. The confessions of those who stood trial inevitably implicated others, who in turn implicated others, and so on. Ordinary party workers were soon caught up in this mass purging and the confessions of lower officials led to their bosses being brought in for interrogation. A similar process occurred at the top, as leaders were arrested and those who worked for them were caught up in the whirlwind. The numbers of those purged from the higher echelons of the party show how devastating this 'cleansing' was. Of

139 members of the party Central Committee elected at the 'Congress of Victors' in 1934, 110 had been arrested by the time of the 1939 Congress. Delegates at the 1934 Congress were also targeted: 1,108 of them were arrested out of 1,961. Leading party officials throughout the Soviet Union were now often viewed with suspicion as potential threats to Stalin, and leaders at the state level within the Soviet republics were also removed. This was a widespread, bloody reorganisation of the party from the top down and the bottom up. Few were safe: hundreds of thousands of Communists were purged. It quickly became clear that anyone who could possibly be perceived as a threat to Stalin's position was at risk.

Why did these Bolsheviks, who had played such important roles in the history of the Soviet Union, confess to such outlandish and unlikely crimes? The most obvious reason is that they were forced to. The NKVD used extreme coercive methods in its Lubyanka headquarters and threatened to harm the families of the accused as well. Interrogation could involve sleep and food deprivation as well as physical torture. It is little wonder that so many accepted that they were guilty of something. However, others saw confession as a personal vindication of their lives. They had devoted years to the cause of revolutionary socialism, their life's work stood before them in the shape of the USSR, supposedly the beacon for socialism throughout the world. If they did not confess to their 'crimes' they would have been opposing Stalin, the living embodiment of the socialist dream. Therefore many Communists, such as Bukharin, accepted their guilt as part of the continuation of the struggle for socialism. In December 1937, just before his execution, Bukharin wrote to Stalin. In his letter he said that '*great* plans, *great* ideas and *great* interests take precedence over everything. And I know that it would be petty of me to place the question of my own person *on a par* with the *universal-historical* tasks resting…on your shoulders.' To accept that the party might be perverting the Communist dream would mean that their struggle had been meaningless and that their faith in a better world had been deeply misplaced.

Andrei Vyshinsky concluded the final show trial in his usual fashion. He declared that the road to communism had been cleared of the 'last scum and filth of the past'. The Soviet people could now 'march ever onward, toward communism' with 'our beloved leader and teacher, the great Stalin, at our head'. The speeches and confessions were published in newspapers, to ensure that the population were fully aware of the party's success. Public meetings were held where workers demanded the death sentence for these traitors to the Soviet cause. In some cases, the Purges were seen as something that was just happening to 'them', the leaders at the top. This view changed when the party widened its attacks to incorporate the rest of society.

As enemies had been found at the highest and lowest levels of the Communist Party, it seemed logical, at least to Stalin and the NKVD, that more anti-Soviet elements could be active in the wider society. This ensured that the purging of the party spread to the rest of the system and ultimately attacked ordinary Soviet citizens in what is known as the 'Great Terror'. Millions were affected by arrests, deportations, long sentences in the gulag, and executions. This was already a time of great fear and paranoia, as a war with Nazi Germany looked increasingly likely. Fascist agents and Nazi sympathisers were supposedly around every corner and were to blame for acts of sabotage that could threaten the USSR's capability to defend itself against a foreign invasion.

Attacking Soviet society: the Terror widens

Until mid-1937, repression had largely been directed against Communist Party members. However, the search for enemies of the state then turned to the higher levels of other parts of the system. NKVD members, including its head, Genrikh Yagoda, were purged, as was the Red Army. Senior military figures, such as the hero of the Russian Civil War, Marshal Mikhail Tukhachevsky, were purged and executed in a secret trial overseen by Stalin. He saw the spectre of an army coup looming and had many more officers sent to the gulag, severely depleting the Soviet forces that would have to resist Hitler just a few years later. Administrators, managers and the intelligentsia were also purged and many victims spent years in camps such as those in Kolyma in the Russian Far East.

On 28 June 1937 the Politburo sought to widen the search for 'counter-revolutionary' forces. Its attention now turned to the insurrectionary organisations among exiled kulaks in Western Siberia. The Politburo ordered the shooting of anyone found guilty of such activities and this, according to Oleg Khlevnyuk, heralded a new stage in the purges. A *troika* (three-person tribunal) consisting of the regional party secretary and NKVD chief and a procurator was established which could bypass the normal judicial procedure and thus ensure quick results. Within a few days these committees were extended to the whole country.

More Politburo resolutions followed as Stalin and his comrades grew fearful of anti-Communist opposition among those they had exiled, noting that 'the majority of former kulaks and criminals, who were exiled…have returned to their *oblast*' [region] [and] are the main instigators of all kinds of anti-Soviet…crimes.' Stalin sent telegrams to the local authorities demanding that 'enemies' be shot without question and approving the use of torture as a means of getting confessions. On 30 July the Politburo ratified the NKVD's Order No. 00447 which targeted 'former kulaks, criminals and other anti-Soviet elements', setting a 'norm' of 75,000 people to be shot and 225,000 to be sent to the camps. This target was fulfilled at least twice: the numbers required for arrest and execution were agreed before the victims had been found. The NKVD's reach extended far beyond the Communist Party, although their activities still remained largely concentrated in the cities rather than in the countryside. The *Yezhovshchina* now cast its net more widely, targeting millions of ordinary people in a violent assault on other areas of the Soviet system. Various ethnic groups were included in the NKVD's offensive and specific categories of foreign citizens living in the USSR found themselves victims of 'national sweeps'. Eastern Europeans, especially Poles, were seen as potential enemies along with Koreans, Chinese and Germans. It was assumed that they might have maintained links with, or loyalty to, their former countries and this could not be tolerated in a system where all loyalty went to the Soviet state and its leader.

NKVD Order No. 00485, approved by the Politburo in August 1937, saw a 'Polish Operation' arrest 140,000 people, 110,000 of them being shot. Three years later, in the Katyn massacre, the Soviet authorities shot dead more than 20,000 Polish officers and prisoners of war, all of whom came under Soviet jurisdiction after the signing of the Nazi–Soviet pact in August 1939. British and American Communists, however, were often not arrested, evidence that this 'cleansing' of foreign Communists was to some extent centrally directed. This new all-embracing policy was confirmed in November 1937, when Stalin spoke ominously of destroying all 'sworn' enemies of the USSR, i.e. anyone who sought 'to destroy the unity of the socialist state'. At a private celebration to mark the twentieth anniversary of the Bolshevik revolution, Stalin said that any such enemy would be destroyed, 'even if he is an Old Bolshevik'. He made it clear that any opposition, even in the minds of the people, would not be tolerated and declared that anyone who threatened the 'unity of the socialist state, either in deed or in thought — yes, even in thought — will be mercilessly destroyed'. This statement was taken to its chilling, logical conclusion by including anyone who had ever previously opposed Soviet rule.

Attention now turned to former members of other political parties, such as the Mensheviks and Socialist Revolutionaries, and any others who had once struggled against the Soviet state. Kulaks, White Guards, political prisoners and surviving tsarist officials were to be arrested and either shot or sent to the gulag for 8 to 10 years. Moscow ordered that quotas (*limity*) were to be fulfilled. This gave the Terror a particular rationale: the NKVD justified its position by reference to the number of enemies in existence, which in turn encouraged it to keep uncovering enemies. In an odd twist to the NKVD operations, people who had been arrested would sometimes meet their arresting agent in the camps after he had been detained for not fulfilling his quota and thus becoming 'politically suspect'.

We know that victims of Moscow's cleansing of the system could also include the families of 'enemies of the people'. One such family member was Nina Lugovskaya, whose diaries turned up in the NKVD archives and were published in 2003 under the title *I Want to Live*. Nina's father, who had once been a Socialist Revolutionary, was arrested and exiled and, since her father was treated with suspicion, so too was Nina. Her diary reflects the difficulty of growing up as a normal teenager in Stalin's Moscow while coping with the growing Stalinist system which kept her apart from her father. She wrote about experiences ranging from life in school and going to parties to raging against Stalin for taking her father away from her ('I dreamt for hours about how I would kill him…the vile Georgian who is crippling Russia'), checking who was at the door before opening it and preparing herself for a visit from the Soviet authorities.

Nina's diary entry for 2 November 1932 describes a visit from two uniformed men and two Red Army officers. After asking who was at the door and being told 'the janitor', she realised what was happening 'but there was still a vague hope left somewhere in my heart'. Surveillance and police raids, together with the midnight call from the NKVD, were key features of the Purges and a useful way of instilling fear into people.

Another characteristic of this period was the denunciation of ordinary Soviet citizens by others. Some people joined in for personal gain: it was a good way of removing a troublesome neighbour or a corrupt or spiteful boss. Others did it for ideological reasons, genuinely believing that someone posed a threat to the Communist cause; these have been termed 'loyalty denunciations'. It has been said that denunciation was a 'weapon of the weak': Communists and non-Communists alike had few other ways of fighting back against a system that treated them so poorly. Denouncing managers carried some risk: if a worker complained to the higher authorities and the complaint was returned to the local level, the complainant might be the one to suffer rather than the boss.

This gave the Purges and the Terror another dynamic, a force from below, which the leaders in Moscow interpreted as evidence of the very enemies they claimed were everywhere. At times, the chaotic nature of local politics meant that orders from the centre were not implemented in some regions, and this led Moscow to impose more severe measures. At other times, this chaos could mean that the centre was actually unaware of arrests and terror outside Moscow, as local party leaders used central directives to settle old scores with local enemies. Some ordinary people made use of the suspicious atmosphere to remove their own rivals or bugbears, who could include the local party secretary.

When reading about the hardships of people like Nina Lugovskaya or of how neighbour would denounce neighbour, there is a tendency to accept that this was the experience shared by everyone in Stalin's Soviet Union, a view of Soviet life that was accepted in the West for decades. It is still widely believed that no-one was safe from the infamous midnight call from Stalin's NKVD, and stories of how people kept packed bags by their front doors in case of such a call were seen as evidence of how ordinary Soviet citizens were also targets for the secret police. However, the questions of how widespread the terror was and whether or not Soviet citizens lived in a permanent state of fear during the 1930s are still hotly debated by historians, who have been unable to reach any conclusive agreement.

While the Purges were clearly devastating and eliminated hundreds of thousands of Communists, army personnel, NKVD agents, national leaders and ethnic groups, the Terror may not have touched everyone either directly or even indirectly. For many years it was assumed that everyone knew someone who had spent time in the gulag or at least knew of someone who had been taken away by the NKVD. However, Christopher Read (2003, p. 103) notes that 'the impact of the purges was very variable. The elites of the metropolises suffered more directly than the workers of Magnitogorsk. The rural collective farm peasantry was little affected.' Kevin McDermott (2006, p. 102) disagrees with this, claiming that 'in strictly numerical terms the bulk of those repressed did not come from the elites, but were "ordinary" non-Communist citizens, "kulaks," workers…the homeless…all those who deviated from the social norms of the Stalinist "utopia"'.

Taking the debate still further, Robert Thurston has even argued, admittedly controversially, that most Soviet citizens led relatively normal lives and that the Purges did not cause the widespread fear that advocates of the totalitarian thesis claim. Thurston claims that people's reactions to arrests suggested that there was no general fear in the 1930s: it was only those who were actually arrested who realised that innocent citizens were being widely persecuted. Those who remained outside the NKVD's clutches often accepted that those arrested must have done something that deserved arrest. Thurston also denies that there was any such feeling that 'anyone could be next'. Read (2003, p. 104) concurs, noting that 'even the Purges did not create a universal atmosphere of fear and obedience'.

It is still difficult to ascertain exactly how widespread the Terror was, but it is worth noting the problems of 'collective memory' when searching for historical 'truths'. Mary McAuley gives an excellent example of this problem when she describes interviewing a woman in her eighties about her experience of the Purges. Having established that the woman lived in a communal apartment, where she shared a kitchen and bathroom with ten families, McAuley notes that her response when asked how many people she knew who were arrested in 1937 would be one of 'wide-eyed amazement':

> 'Haven't you read Solzhenitsyn? Don't you know that *everyone* was arrested?' If you continue with: 'But were any of your family arrested?', there may well be a pause…'Well, no, not in my family, but everybody else was.' Then you ask: 'How many people were arrested in the communal apartment you lived in?' There's a very long pause, followed by 'Well, hmm, I don't really remember, but yes, yes, there was one, Ivanov, who lived at the room down at the end, yes, now I remember.' (quoted in Ward 1999, p. 136)

This story adds weight to the argument that not everyone was touched by Stalin's repression. The Terror may have been widespread in certain areas but not everyone had a direct experience of it.

Conclusion

As 1938 drew to a close, the Terror subsided. Just as he had during collectivisation, Stalin blamed the excessive nature of the Purges on the failings of others, most noticeably Yezhov. Beria replaced him as head of the NKVD and Yezhov, the man who had done so much damage to the country, was himself purged, becoming one of the last victims of Stalin's Terror. After pleading for his life Yezhov was executed in 1940. He asked that Stalin be told, 'I shall die with his name upon my lips.'

Since the opening of the Soviet archives there has been a reassessment of the number of victims of the Purges. The frighteningly high figures have been revised downwards, with the suggestion that the original figures may themselves have been exaggerated. Accounts written during the Cold War confidently stated that Stalin killed millions of his own people at the height of the Terror; more recent research suggests that closer to 1 million people (approximately 900,000) were shot for 'counter-revolutionary crimes' between the mid-1930s and Stalin's death in 1953. The numbers of inmates in the camps peaked at around 4 million by the end of the 1930s, with between 55,000 and 75,000 deaths there during the purge years. These figures include criminals as well as political prisoners.

This does not mean that the Purges and Terror were any less devastating for those caught up in this terrifying attack on the Soviet population, but it does suggest that the numbers of those who fell victim to this Stalinist 'whirlwind' were lower than originally assumed. However, even if fewer lives were lost or affected than initially thought, we can still see that one person gained from the overall process and that, of course, was Stalin. He had allowed virtual civil war in the party between 1936 and 1938, and he benefited as his main rivals, past and present, were permanently removed. Although the Purges and Terror to some extent took on a life of their own in the regions, the fear felt by many Soviet citizens and the stress and emotional hardship experienced by ordinary people trying to survive in a rapidly changing world were ultimately consequences of Stalin's own terrible actions.

Questions

1 To what extent does the historical debate on the Great Terror come down to squabbling over numbers?

2 In what ways was the NKVD itself a victim of the Terror? Can the same be said for Stalin?

3 On the basis of the evidence about the Soviet Union in the 1930s, in what ways can a country be accurately described as existing in a 'state of terror'?

References

- McDermott, K. (2006) *Stalin: Revolutionary in an Era of War*, Palgrave Macmillan.
- Read, C. (ed.) (2003) *The Stalin Years: A Reader*, Palgrave Macmillan.
- Ward, C. (1999) *Stalin's Russia*, Arnold.

Stalin: creator or destroyer?

When Josef Stalin died in March 1953 he left a mixed legacy behind him. He had built a country and system strong enough to withstand the massive Nazi onslaught after Hitler turned his attention eastwards in 1941, but he did it through repression, coercion and murder. This concluding chapter looks at the final years of Stalin's life, including the war, and the immediate post-Stalin years. It assesses his legacy and asks whether he built more than he destroyed and whether any positives can be found in Stalinism.

Stalin as war leader

As if the Soviet population had not been through enough turmoil and tragedy in the 1930s, they then suffered at the hands of Nazi Germany after Hitler's forces invaded the Soviet Union in June 1941. The USSR was forced into the Second World War and became an important ally of Britain and later the USA. Despite some awful decisions made by Stalin, not least his trust of Hitler in spite of years of Nazi anti-Soviet propaganda, the USSR emerged victorious from its struggle against Nazism. However, the price of this victory was the lives of more than 27 million Soviet people and utter devastation between 1941 and 1945.

After the initial Nazi attack in June 1941, which saw more than 5.5 million troops, nearly 3 million tanks and 5,000 aircraft sweep over Leningrad, Moscow and Kiev, a deeply shocked Stalin retreated to his dacha. However, within a couple of weeks he was working tirelessly in the Kremlin to turn things around.

One of the problems facing the Communist Party was that many Soviet citizens had little reason to support the regime. In some areas the Nazis were even welcomed as liberators on the basis that nothing could be as bad as Stalinism, although people soon realised that this was a mistake and most Soviet citizens fought extremely bravely to resist the invaders. Stalin sought to galvanise his people for the long battle ahead. The Russian Orthodox Church was allowed to preach again and became an important means of rallying the many people who had secretly maintained their religious beliefs. Stalin made speeches that relied less on Communist rhetoric and more on patriotic language, calling on his Russian 'brothers and sisters' to defend their country (significantly, not communism) against the German offensive. This was less an ideological war and more a 'Great Patriotic War', as the Second World War is still known in Russia.

Crucially, Stalin remained a visual presence in Moscow throughout the war. He could be seen taking the salute from the roof of Lenin's mausoleum in Red Square on the anniversary of the Bolshevik revolution and people generally believed that he was sharing in their suffering. He proved willing to listen to his army commanders and showed sound tactical knowledge. During a meeting with Winston Churchill in Moscow, the British prime minister was impressed with Stalin's geographical instincts when they discussed the North African campaign. All of these factors helped to solidify people's support for Stalin and the party, helping the USSR to make a massive contribution to the Allies' victory in the war with Nazi Germany.

Debate still rages over Stalin's handling of the immediate pre-war period and the early stages of the war, but Stalin undoubtedly proved a very effective war leader and his wartime record inspired many citizens to feel more positive about him after the war. The war thus proved to be 'Stalin's October', when he was finally able to step out of Lenin's shadow.

Postwar developments

The Stalinist system that was built so quickly and at such heavy human cost in the 1930s came under intense pressure during the war. Tens of millions of people were killed, maimed or made homeless. Cities, villages, industry and agriculture were all destroyed in the carnage. Yet what emerged from the wreckage was a country that found itself as one of two new 'superpowers', the other being the USA, with whom it would spend the next four and a half decades at loggerheads during the Cold War. The international position of the USSR had been enormously enhanced by its war efforts, as had Stalin's domestic standing, and the country now had much greater military and diplomatic strength. This was further enhanced when the USSR exploded its first atomic bomb in 1949, ending the USA's nuclear monopoly. The Kremlin had also extended its control over a vast area of eastern Europe, establishing so-called 'People's Democracies' in countries such as Poland and Czechoslovakia. This extension of Stalinism into mainland Europe saw the establishment of a Kremlin-backed state in East Germany, which provoked fears in the West that communism was once again on the march. Soviet power stretched across more than one sixth of the globe: Stalinism seemed unstoppable.

Inside the Soviet Union, the conservative nature of the period of 'High Stalinism' (1945–53) was confirmed as society became more xenophobic and constrained by the drab ideological norms of the *Zhdanovshchina*, the period dominated by the party's ideological chief, Andrei Zhdanov. Once again Stalinist repression jailed innocent people to ensure that guilty individuals did not roam free. Bizarrely, released Soviet prisoners of war were sent to the labour camps, as it was believed that their 'contact' with non-Soviets (i.e. imprisonment at the hands of the enemy) could be harmful to the Soviet way of life. Red Army officers who had befriended British or American military personnel during the war could be jailed for receiving letters from them. The limited freedoms that had been granted during the war to bodies such as the Church were quickly rescinded as Stalin resumed his total control over the country.

However, by the early 1950s Stalin was old and tired after the years of turmoil and war. He was drinking heavily and he began to withdraw from the day-to-day running of the country. This led to the emergence of factions that became more and more politically dominant in the later stages of his rule. Stalin grew even more suspicious, especially of the increasingly hostile West once the Cold War was under way. Domestically, he deeply distrusted the citizens of Leningrad who had fought so bravely and, because of the crippling 900-day siege of their city, largely independently during the war. This led to the 'Leningrad Affair' which saw important party figures, including Politburo member Nikolai Voznesensky, executed without a fair trial. A fabricated 'Doctors' Plot' alleged that Jewish doctors were either poisoning or planning to poison the Soviet leaders, including Zhdanov, who had died in 1948. Repression and terror were still central to Stalin's system and there were rumours that another round of purges would soon begin.

The culture of fear and suspicion took a final ironic twist on 1 March 1953, when it ensured that the dying Soviet dictator did not receive the medical attention he desperately needed. Stalin had failed to come out of his room in his dacha by midday, which was late even for him. His staff and security guards were too scared to disturb him, even though there was obvious cause for concern. Finally, late in the evening, his door was opened and Stalin was found lying on his sofa in a semi-coma having had a stroke. His Politburo comrades were called from Moscow, although Beria did not arrive until the early hours of the following morning. Having checked the leader's condition for himself, Beria, by then head of the MVD (the Ministry of Internal Affairs, a department which included the former NKVD), declared that Stalin was simply in a deep sleep. He dismissed the concerns of the others and left the dacha. It was only after Beria's return at 9 a.m. that the doctors were allowed in to see the General Secretary, a delay that Stalin's daughter Svetlana Alliluyeva believed led to her father's death. His condition deteriorated over the next few days and at 9.50 on the night of 5 March, Josef Stalin died.

In various parts of the Soviet empire, the immediate and understandable reaction was one of joy that the dictator was gone for ever; anti-Stalinist riots broke out in the gulag, where inmates seized this opportunity to protest their innocence. Nevertheless, amidst the predictable state-sponsored mourning that brought millions onto the streets of Russia to weep at the death of the *vozhd'*, there was genuine grief. After his funeral, Stalin was placed alongside Lenin in the Red Square mausoleum, where Soviet citizens could file past quietly and pay their respects to their former leader. No doubt some went simply to make sure he was dead.

At the time of Stalin's death in 1953, the USSR was in a far stronger position in the world than it had been in the 1930s. As Isaac Deutscher, one of Stalin's biographers, described it, the Soviet dictator had found the USSR with a plough and left it with a nuclear bomb. This is certainly one way of viewing Stalin's legacy, as one of successful modernisation that had begun at a time when the Great Depression was devastating the people and economies of the West. After the war, Soviet power extended into eastern and central Europe. The Kremlin's influence was also felt in other areas of the globe, not least in Korea, where a war between the north and south of the country saw the USSR support Communist North Korea while the USA aided capitalist South Korea. Under Stalin's leadership, the Soviet Union became a superpower that went on to rival the USA for nearly 50 years.

Inside the USSR, Stalin bequeathed a highly personalised political system. The dictatorship of the party had become the dictatorship of Stalin, and the NKVD to a large extent was Stalin's personal secret police. The Communist Party was now a Stalinist party, in which the leader had the power of life and death over his comrades. It was a system that was based on terror and oppression, where the penalties for people indulging in independent thought or resisting party orders ranged from losing their jobs to losing their freedom or even their lives. Stalin centralised control and amassed a huge amount of power around himself and his closest comrades, thus ensuring that power flowed from the centre to the periphery, from the top to the bottom.

Stalin's power was nothing like total in the 'totalitarian' sense of the word. There were still challenges to his power inside the party, while agencies such as the NKVD and pressure for change from workers influenced proceedings at the top more than those from the totalitarian school have ever believed possible. This is not to suggest that Stalin's word was not final, but rather that Soviet political and social life were determined by more than Stalin's will alone. This meant that whoever took over from Stalin as leader of the Soviet Union would need to address crucial questions concerning political power and control, two key aspects of his legacy. However, the more immediate questions were who should assume power and, perhaps more interestingly, who *could* replace the 'wise leader and teacher of the Communist Party and of the Soviet people', as Stalin was described in the radio broadcast announcing his death.

After Stalin

With no mechanism in place to ensure a smooth transition to Stalin's successor, a power struggle followed his death, just as it had after Lenin's. The main candidates were Georgy Malenkov, Nikita Khrushchev and Vyacheslav Molotov. Lavrenty Beria, the feared head of the secret police, also hoped to take over from Stalin, but the other leading figures, fearful that he would purge them from the party, quickly removed him from his position. Beria was accused of attempting a coup and denounced as a British spy, both of which charges were false. He was arrested and shot at the end of 1953. His death was of great significance because it was the last political execution in the Soviet Union.

The ending of a system based on terror was the first major attempt to reform Stalinism. Although the Soviet Union retained political repression as a means of control for the rest of its existence, it moved away from what Mark Sandle has called 'institutionalised mass terror' (Sandle 1999, p. 282). This was one of the first challenges to Stalin's legacy, and it proved to be one of the most important. The power of the secret police was downgraded and it was brought under the direct control of the Communist Party of the Soviet Union (CPSU). It was renamed the Committee for State Security (KGB) in 1954, but was henceforth subordinate to the Central Committee of the Communist Party and its head was appointed by the party. The KGB only had the power to investigate and arrest, not to try, a suspect and it lost control of the administration of the labour camps, which were now controlled by the Ministry of Justice. The camps themselves underwent a dramatic change: millions of inmates were released from them within a few years of Stalin's death. This was a highly significant, if partial, dismantling of the Stalinist legacy of the police state.

The fight for control of the post-Stalinist Soviet Union saw challenges to other aspects of Stalin's legacy and a cautious relaxation of Stalinist norms. Loyal Stalinists such as Molotov advocated continuing with Stalin's belligerent approach, especially in foreign policy, but the more reform-minded Malenkov and Khrushchev hoped to take the country down a different, less extreme, path. This did not mean fundamentally altering the basic structure of the Soviet state, but it did mean ending some of Stalin's excesses.

Nevertheless, moderates in the Soviet leadership had to consider how far they could go without seriously threatening the power and stability of the state. For example, Malenkov favoured shifting the emphasis in economic policy away from heavy industry, the basis of Soviet construction during the 1930s, towards consumer goods; he also supported a less aggressive foreign policy. The Foreign Minister, Molotov, opposed this new line, which he dubbed 'peaceful co-existence', but found himself sidelined by Malenkov and Khrushchev. Khrushchev hoped for some kind of reconciliation with the Yugoslav Communist leader, Josip Tito; his platform included a preference for heavy industry, although he was also pro-agriculture. This power struggle allowed for some of the central pillars of the Stalinist system to be questioned: economic priorities, foreign policy and the role of the secret police were all scrutinised and challenged, as reformist leaders sought to shape the country along distinctly post-Stalinist lines, even if they used Stalinist tactics to do so.

Khrushchev gradually outmanoeuvred Malenkov, forcing him to choose between being prime minister or General Secretary of the Communist Party. As the party had been reduced in importance under Stalin, Malenkov chose the premiership, leaving Khrushchev to become General Secretary. This proved a grave mistake: Khrushchev purged over half the party's local and regional secretaries and replaced them with his own supporters. The new General Secretary was using Stalinist methods to move the USSR on from Stalinism.

Ironically, just as Trotsky, rather than Stalin, had been seen by many as the natural successor to Lenin, so Malenkov, rather than Khrushchev, was seen as the most obvious choice to succeed Stalin. Yet by 1955 Malenkov had been replaced as prime minister by Nikolai Bulganin, who had been recruited by Khrushchev to help in the fight against Beria. By February 1956 Khrushchev's supreme position in the Soviet system was assured and his time in the Kremlin was characterised to a large extent by his attempts to de-Stalinise the country. It was in February 1956 that Khrushchev launched a devastating assault on Stalin's legacy in what is known as his 'Secret Speech', a 4-hour-long address to a closed session of the Communist Party's Twentieth Congress, in which he condemned Stalin for abusing his power from 1934 onwards (the date was possibly carefully chosen to implicate Stalin in the murder of Kirov).

Khrushchev needed to consolidate his position as head of the party and of the USSR and he did this by attacking his former master. He accused Stalin of fostering a cult of personality and falsifying history, and denounced him for victimising innocent people, leading the murderous Purges and presiding over the decline of the party. The irony was that, as head of the Ukrainian party, Khrushchev had done Stalin's bidding during the Purges. These revelations shocked those present at the congress. Some could not accept that Stalin was guilty, while others were scared that their roles in these events would be discovered. Despite its being a 'secret' speech in the sense that the press were not present, details soon spread around the world via delegates from the international Communist parties who were in attendance and it had a huge impact on how Stalin and the Soviet Union were perceived by Communists and non-Communists alike. Many staunch supporters of Stalin and the USSR found it difficult to continue believing in him.

Stalin's legacy

There are two questions that must be asked when assessing Stalin's legacy: what changed when Stalin was in power and what were the consequences of his rule? We will deal with these two questions together.

When assessing the changes to the USSR under Stalin it is difficult not to conclude that Stalin left behind a radically different country from the one he inherited in the 1920s. The semi-capitalism of the NEP years was replaced by a planned economic experiment, a vast programme of industrial and agricultural reconstruction which totally changed the USSR's social, economic and political infrastructure. Although this did not lead to the creation of a socialist system that Marx and Lenin would have recognised, it did produce a planned economy with no unemployment at a time when lack of work cursed the lives of millions in Europe and the USA.

The emphasis on heavy industry ensured that the country was in a position to defend itself against Hitler's forces. The importance of this should not be underestimated: without industrialisation the USSR could not have been so successful in its fight against fascism. Of course, this economic rebuilding came at a very high price, in terms of people's suffering. The workers lived in crowded, hastily built homes and laboured in factories where conditions were as dire as they had been during western Europe's industrialisation in the nineteenth century.

The peasants were treated brutally. They were herded onto collective farms and ordered to deliver what the state needed, despite the fact that this often came at the expense of their own needs. Peasants' desperate pleas for food and help during the 1932–33 famine were at best ignored by the central leadership, whose focus was on the proletariat, and at worst dismissed as anti-Communist lies by a government that was enthusiastically trying to 'break the backs of the peasantry' and kill off Ukrainian nationalism.

Politically, the Soviet Communist Party was weakened under Stalin. Whereas Lenin had seen it as the vanguard of the proletariat, Stalin relegated it to a secondary position below himself and his closest comrades. It can even be argued that during the 1930s the party was less important than the NKVD. This does not mean that the party was an irrelevance; it was impossible to get on in the system without being a party member, and party propaganda, enforced through visual media such as art and film, in written forms such as literature, newspapers and textbooks, and through active participation in party organisations such as the Komsomol, was an integral part of the Soviet system. A 'New Soviet Person' was supposedly being born and the party was one of its midwives.

However, other institutional forces, notably the NKVD, exerted important influence on the development of Stalinism. These agencies helped to shape the political nature of the system, which suggests that Stalin was not as all-powerful as the totalitarian school claims. Certainly he had more power than anyone else, including the power of life and death, but he could not be omnipotent in a country the size of, and as underdeveloped as, the USSR. However, the fact that the party had active members, spies and 'little Stalins' in all areas of the country helped to perpetuate this official, though false, view of the *vozhd'* and the party.

Socially, Stalin delivered great benefits for some and great suffering for many. This is true of many political systems; the point here is that there was such a huge difference between the two. Upwardly mobile workers (*vydvizhentsy*) found themselves in positions of responsibility that would not have been possible during tsarism. Their new roles brought a better standard of living, which in turn contributed to the development of a more conservative brand of Stalinism: those who had gained from the system wanted to safeguard their position. However, *vydvizhentsy* often received their positions at the expense of others and it was always possible that they too could become victims of the Stalinist system.

Despite apparent positives, such as the vast industrialisation programme that saved the country during the war and the improved living standards enjoyed by certain groups, no conclusion on Stalin's legacy can ignore the terribly high number of victims of his system. The famine of 1932–33 saw between 5 and 6 million lives lost; even with figures revised downwards from their Cold War high of 20 million deaths, the Purges and Great Terror saw millions of innocent people persecuted, incarcerated and murdered at the hands of the Stalinist state. Suffering is always likely when new political, religious and social orders are brought into existence, but under Stalin there were too many times when this was deliberate and vicious.

The system that Stalin created lasted until the mid-1980s, when Mikhail Gorbachev became General Secretary of the CPSU and began to alter the fundamental socioeconomic and political structure of the Soviet Union through his policy of *perestroika* (restructuring). Until then, the USSR retained the basic Stalinist structure, while losing some of its key features: this long survival was one of Stalin's main legacies. The Soviet Union's authoritarian bureaucracy outlived its founder by moving away from some Stalinist norms, such as terror, while keeping others, such as repression. The Stalinist planned economy embraced consumerism as much as was possible within this post-Stalin political setting.

Even today, some Russian towns erect statues in Stalin's honour. In December 2005, residents of the southern Russian town of Digora showed off their new statue of Stalin to commemorate the anniversary of his birth. Such overt pro-Stalinism is not common practice and those who remember Stalin fondly probably either benefited from his rule or have not benefited in the new post-Gorbachev Russia. Although Stalin proved a 'modernising tsar', his modernisation came at a terrible price. His methods brought death and destruction to millions of Soviet citizens and oppression to the countries of eastern Europe. Stalin achieved his aim of creating a strong and secure Soviet Union, but he destroyed the lives of so many innocents in so many ways to get there.

Questions

1 How well can Stalin be compared as a war leader with his allies, Roosevelt and Churchill?
2 To what extent did Khrushchev's de-Stalinisation follow Stalinist practices?
3 How fair is it to say that Stalinism was at its most successful after Stalin's death?

Reference

- Sandle, M. (1999) *A Short History of Soviet Socialism*, Routledge.

Looking at documents and pictures

Documentary analysis

The need for rapid industrialisation

It is sometimes asked whether it is not possible to slow down the tempo (of industrialisation) a bit, to put a check on the movement. No, comrades, it is not possible! The tempo must not be reduced! On the contrary, we must increase it as much as is within our powers and possibilities. This is dictated to us by our obligations to the workers and peasants of the USSR. This is dictated to us by our obligations to the working class of the whole world.

To slacken the tempo would mean falling behind. And those who fall behind get beaten. But we do not want to be beaten. No, we refuse to be beaten! One feature of the history of old Russia was the continual beatings she suffered for falling behind, for her backwardness.

She was beaten by the British and French capitalists. She was beaten by the Japanese barons. All beat her — for her backwardness: for military backwardness, for cultural backwardness, for political backwardness, for industrial backwardness, for agricultural backwardness. She was beaten because to do so was profitable and could be done with impunity…. Such is the law of the exploiters — to beat the backward and the weak. It is the jungle law of capitalism. You are backward, you are weak — therefore you are wrong; hence you can be beaten and enslaved. You are mighty — therefore you are right; hence, we must be wary of you.

That is why we must no longer lag behind.

In the past we had no fatherland, nor could we have one. But now that we have overthrown capitalism and power is in the hands of the working class, we have a fatherland, and we will defend its independence. Do you want our Socialist fatherland to be beaten and to lose its independence? If you do not want this you must put an end to its backwardness in the shortest possible time and develop genuine Bolshevik tempo in building up its Socialist system of economy. There is no other way. That is why Lenin said during the October Revolution: 'Either perish, or overtake and outstrip the advanced capitalist countries.'

We are 50 or 100 years behind the advanced countries. We must make good this distance in 10 years. Either we do it, or they crush us.

Stalin, J. V. (1931) *The Tasks of Business Executives* (extracts),
from *Leninism* (1940), Lawrence & Wishart.

Stalin gave this speech (also referred to as 'The Tasks of the Economic Executives') to the first All-Union Congress of Managers of Socialist Industry, held in 1931. The speech is excellent evidence not only of Stalin's priorities in the early 1930s but also of the fears and concerns that shaped his thoughts throughout the decade. For much of the speech he spoke of the 'economic tasks' that were ahead for those involved in the newly industrialising Soviet economy. However, the extracts above highlight reasons why Stalin thought it necessary to industrialise over and above the economic needs of the country.

The first point to note is the emphasis he places on speed. During the post-Leninist power struggle Trotsky declared that the USSR should industrialise rapidly, whereas Stalin preferred to ally with Bukharin, who advocated a slower tempo for industrial development. Towards the end of the decade, however, Stalin changed his mind and adopted Trotsky's idea. In this document Stalin states clearly that the Soviet Union must not slacken the immense pace of modernisation; indeed, he insists that the tempo should be increased as much as possible.

There were two reasons for this demand. The first was Stalin's desire for a more modern, less backward Russia. This fed into the second reason for rapid change: Stalin's belief that hostile forces were gathering outside the USSR and were preparing to attack the country. This belief explains his comments about falling behind and getting beaten by the West. As he looked to a strong Soviet state in the future he rejected the 'old Russia' of the past which had 'suffered because of her backwardness'. This new Soviet 'Fatherland' would no longer be threatened by old external enemies such as the 'British and French capitalists...the Japanese barons', nor by old internal 'enemies' such as military, cultural, political, industrial and agricultural backwardness. With this in mind, the attack on the Communist Party during the Purges and the attack on the population during the Terror may be seen as a logical extension of the policy of safeguarding the security both of Stalin and of the Soviet Union.

This document highlights the fact that the Soviet Union during Stalin's rule was obsessed with creating a modern country safe from internal and external threats: modernity and security were two of the main themes of Stalinism, and were pursued regardless of the human cost. Stalin is concerned that unless the

USSR catches up with the capitalist powers, they 'will crush us'. Interestingly, this passage has been translated in different ways ('they crush us'; 'we shall be crushed'; 'we go under'), a useful reminder that the original can take on different shades of meaning depending on who is translating it.

The Tasks of Business Executives shows some of Stalin's fears, which were ultimately shared by the party and then by parts of the system and society. It also emphasises Stalin's desire for modernisation and demonstrates that his reasons for wanting to build a strong country came from insecurity and paranoia, two dangerous factors when combined within a political context.

Picture analysis

1 Stalin with Communist Party comrades

David King Collection

This picture shows Josef Stalin standing with his Communist Party comrades Grigory Ordzhonikidze, Kliment Voroshilov and Valerian Kuibyshev to his right, and Mikhail Kalinin, Lazar Kaganovich and Sergei Kirov to his left. It was taken in the Kremlin on 21 December 1929 at the celebrations for Stalin's fiftieth birthday. The presence of Lenin's statue is significant, as it acts as a useful reminder that his role in death was as an ever-present watcher over his 'disciples', the most loyal of whom was, of course, the central figure here, Josef

Stalin. It is also important to remember that this semi-religious approach where Lenin was concerned entirely contradicted his atheism.

The photograph implies a continuation with 'Leninism' (which was a Stalinist construct anyway), but the birthday celebrations in fact marked an important break with it, as it is generally accepted that this was the first time that the word *vozhd'* was used in reference to Stalin. Although the word is generally translated as 'leader', it took on a much greater meaning when used to refer to Stalin and could be likened to the German word Führer. For Stalin, who was supposedly constructing an egalitarian society, it came to mean 'first among equals', thus undermining the hopes and ideals of the 1917 revolution.

2 Stalin with a group of Soviet children

David King Collection

Art, posters and flags were an important means by which the Kremlin conveyed pro-Soviet messages to the people. For some years after the revolution the USSR was a country where many people could not read, and this meant that visual images were crucial to the success of Soviet propaganda.

This picture of Stalin with a group of Soviet children is an excellent example of the kind of positive images that the Communist Party wanted to put across. It was painted in 1936, the year when the first show trial took place and Stalin turned against his old comrades in the party. It shows a benevolent leader surrounded by smiling children offering their 'thanks to beloved Stalin for our happy childhood'. The Stalin in this picture was the caring father of the nation's children, who here represent the various republics of the USSR. The boy in the sailor's uniform carrying a toy boat, and the plane being 'flown' by the girl are reminders that the USSR was becoming a strong, modern and industrialised nation.

The setting is Moscow's Gorky Park, which itself was supposed to be an example of progress brought about by Stalinism, and the leafy green and sky-blue backdrop reminds people that, officially, this was a time of joyous living when life had improved. In Stalin's Russia, Stalin cared for *all* the children, and they in turn were expected to love him more than their own parents.

Bibliography

S. Davies and J. Harris, *Stalin: A New History* (2005)

This is an excellent collection of essays that brings together some of the latest research on different aspects of Stalin and Stalinism. The essays come from papers given at a conference held specially to mark 50 years since the dictator's death. It offers a clear rebuff to those who would reduce the significance of the *vozhd'*:

> ...it is now indisputable that in many respects his [Stalin's] influence was decisive. A clearer understanding of his significance will allow more precise analysis of the origins and nature of Stalinism itself.

J. Arch Getty and O. Naumov, *The Road to Terror: Stalin and the Self-Destruction of the Bolsheviks, 1932–1939* (1999)

Getty is one of the most important of the revisionist historians of Stalin's Russia and this work makes use of nearly 200 documents recently released from the Soviet archives to assess how the Great Terror spread so widely, and to look at both Stalin's role and the role of others in the process. Without in any way diminishing Stalin's importance, the authors stress that he was not working alone:

> Stalin was the central person in the politics and political violence of the 1930s. But his was not the only or even perhaps the most interesting role in the tragedy.

K. McDermott, *Stalin: Revolutionary in an Era of War* (2006)

This recent biography of Stalin is very readable, incorporating new research with new and standard interpretations of Stalin in a lively and enlightening way. This extract gives an idea of the style:

> How...should the historian evaluate a man who consciously shrouded himself in secrecy and fostered a mythic 'cult of personality', who created multiple identities for himself, who has many achievements to his name, but also metaphorically oceans of blood on his hands?

S. Sebag Montefiore, *Stalin: The Court of the Red Tsar* (2003)

This huge and popular biography makes use of the author's access to the Soviet archives and adds valuable details to our understanding of Stalin's personal and political relationships, allowing a more 'human', but no less terrible, Stalin to emerge. The clue to Montefiore's approach lies in the book's title, as this extract shows:

> This is a chronicle of his [Stalin's] court from his acclamation as 'the leader' in 1929 to his death. It is a biography of his courtiers, a study of high politics and informal power and customs. In a way, this is a biography of Stalin himself through his relationships with his magnates: he is never off-stage.

C. Read (ed.), *The Stalin Years: A Reader* (2003)

Chris Read has been one of the most useful writers on Stalin in recent years, collating and analysing the range of views historians have taken. This edited collection of essays offers some excellent insights into Stalin and Stalinism from many leading scholars. There is a useful 'mini-introduction' at the start of each section that helps place the essays in their context. Read explains the reasoning behind his book:

> There is…still a great deal of work to be done but the ongoing research of the post-Soviet period has already begun to illuminate many dark areas and even to change some of the wider contours of our view of the Stalin years.

C. Ward, *Stalin's Russia* (1999)

This is a well-written overview of the main schools of thought on Stalin and Stalinism. It offers a very helpful narrative and an excellent analysis of the historiographical debates.

> Every historian stands to gain from the USSR's collapse, but changes will not come automatically. In order to free themselves academics will have to forget old quarrels and abandon old habits of thought. The history of Stalin's Russia is only just beginning.

Glossary

April Theses

A set of propositions put out by Lenin on his return from exile in April 1917. Proposals included ending support for the Provisional Government and establishing a republic of Soviets.

Bolshevik

The name coined by Lenin for what later became the CPSU (Communist Party of the Soviet Union): from the Russian word for 'majority'.

bureaucracy

The term used to describe the extensive and often stifling administrative system set up by tsarist and Communist Russia.

Caucasian clique

The group of leading Communists, including Budenny and Ordzhonikidze, with roots in Georgia and the Caucasus region, who had a close relationship with Stalin and influence over his decisions.

Central Committee

The main executive body of the Bolshevik, and later Communist, Party. It was not a governmental body.

Cheka

The Bolshevik secret police, named from its Cyrillic initials *Che* and *Ka*.

chistka

A purge, i.e. the arrest and punishment of unreliable members of an organisation.

Civil War

The conflict between the Bolsheviks (the 'Reds') and their various opponents (the 'Whites' and the 'Greens') that followed the October Revolution.

collective farm

Agricultural arrangement whereby land and livestock were held in common and the collective worked according to directions from government.

collectivisation

The process by which the Russian peasants were coerced into abandoning their traditional village landholding communities and moving to a collective farm model.

Comintern

Short for 'Communist International', an organisation representing Communist parties from around the world.

commissar

Originally a political officer attached to military and naval units to ensure political loyalty; the term was also used for all high officers of state.

Commissar for Nationalities

Soviet official responsible for the non-Russian peoples of the Soviet Union.

Communist Party of the Soviet Union (CPSU)

Before the Communist revolution in China in 1949, the CPSU was the undisputed centre of the Communist world. Often referred to in the Soviet Union simply as 'the Party'.

Congress of Victors

Seventeenth Party Congress held in 1934 to mark the success of the first Five-Year Plan.

Council of People's Commissars (Sovnarkom)

The governing body set up in the immediate aftermath of the October Revolution.

CPSU

Communist Party of the Soviet Union.

cult of personality

The policy of showering the leader with excessive personal praise through a widespread programme of propaganda. It ran directly counter to the collectivist principles of the CPSU.

Cultural Revolution

The adaptation of all aspects of Soviet life, especially in the arts and culture, to the demands of Marxism-Leninism and the Soviet state.

dacha

A small country house. Still popular as a weekend retreat for Russian city-dwellers.

Declaration of the 46

Statement by 46 leading Bolsheviks, led by Trotsky, criticising the Politburo and calling for the right to form factions within the CPSU. It was dismissed by Stalin and his supporters as factionalism.

Doctors' Plot
A false accusation in 1952 that a number of Jewish doctors were planning to poison Stalin and other Soviet leaders.

duma
The Russian parliament. The word was used for the assemblies authorised by Tsar Nicholas II and revived for the post-Communist parliaments of the 1990s.

factionalism
Splitting the party into hostile groups or 'factions'. It was outlawed by the Tenth Party Congress in 1921.

Five-Year Plan (*pyatiletka*)
An approach towards accelerating economic growth by rigorous central planning. The first Five-Year Plan ran from 1928 to 1933.

General Secretary of the CPSU
Originally a purely administrative position carrying responsibility for party personnel record-keeping and internal procedures, under Stalin and Khrushchev it became the key governmental position within the Soviet Union.

glasnost
'Openness': the policy of candour in official statements promoted by the government of Mikhail Gorbachev. It resulted in the opening to scholars of the previously closed Soviet archives, notably those covering the Stalin period.

Gosplan
State Committee for Planning, the body that oversaw the Five-Year Plans.

Great Depression
The worldwide economic slump that followed the 1929 Wall Street Crash and the collapse of the US economy.

Great Patriotic War
The name by which Russia's involvement in the Second World War is known in the Soviet Union.

Great Russian chauvinism
Preference for Russians and Russian culture over those of the other national groups of the USSR. Ironically, it was often shown most markedly by those, like Stalin, who were not themselves Russian.

Great Terror

The period of widespread arrests, executions and imprisonment in the gulag sparked off by the murder of Sergei Kirov in 1934.

gulag

Main Administration of Corrective Labour Camps, the state body that administered the Soviet Union's network of labour camps. The term came to be used also for the network itself and for individual camps.

Hero of Labour

An award carrying certain privileges, granted to those who had performed major feats of labour beyond what was expected of them. It was much used during the Five-Year Plans and in the Stakhanovite movement.

internal passport

A device used by the tsarist regime and revived by Stalin to regulate and limit peasant movement within the country.

July Days

Tens of thousands of soldiers, sailors and workers demonstated against the war and the Provisional Government. The Bolshevik leadership failed to give their total support and the uprising was unsuccessful.

KGB

Committee for State Security: secret police force which replaced the NKVD in 1954.

kolkhoz

The Russian word for a collective farm.

Komsomol

Communist Union of Youth, the main Soviet youth movement.

Kronstadt mutiny

Revolt by the men of the Kronstadt naval base near Petrograd in protest at the harsh measures of war communism. It was suppressed and often portrayed, wrongly, as an anti-Bolshevik revolt.

kulak

A rich peasant. In practice the definition was kept loose so that it could be used to label any peasant who resisted state demands.

Left Opposition

Those within the CPSU who opposed the NEP and argued for a rapid drive towards a fully socialist economy and society.

Leningrad Affair

A purge carried out in the late 1940s and early 1950s against leading party members in Leningrad who were accused (falsely) of plotting against Stalin.

Lenin's Testament,

A document drawn up on his deathbed by Lenin, in which he set down his opinion on the personalities of leading Bolsheviks and their suitability for high office. It was generally critical of them, especially of Stalin.

Lubyanka

The headquarters building of the Soviet security forces, successively the *Cheka*, OGPU, NKVD and KGB.

Magnitogorsk

An entire industrial city constructed during the Five-Year Plans in the 1930s. It takes its name from the magnetic mountain on which it was built.

Marxism-Leninism

The offical ideology of the Soviet Union. It was a Stalinist construct that became a part of the cult of Lenin and the cult of Stalin.

Menshevik

Derived from the Russian word for 'minority'. Mensheviks were anti-Bolshevik opponents within the Russian Social Democratic Party (RSDLP) who argued for Russia to progress towards socialism along orthodox Marxist lines. Mensheviks rejected the ideas of Marxism-Leninism.

MTS

Machine Tractor Station. Ostensibly technical centres to help with the mechanisation of Soviet agriculture, these were used by the NKVD as a means of keeping watch on the activities of the peasants.

NEP

New Economic Policy. Announced by Lenin at the Tenth Party Congress in 1921, the NEP allowed for a certain amount of limited capitalist enterprise, especially among peasants, in order to help Russia through the economic difficulties that followed the October Revolution and the Civil War. It proved a highly controversial and deeply divisive policy.

New Soviet Person

The new type of educated, politically aware Soviet citizen that, it was argued, would emerge from Stalin's programme of industrialisation and Cultural Revolution.

NKVD

People's Commissariat for Internal Affairs: the Soviet secret police. In 1954 it was replaced by the KGB.

nomenklatura

A system for promoting those within the party who had shown themselves loyal and reliable. Promotions were sometimes announced by lists. The term was also applied to the people themselves. (From Latin *nomenclatura*, meaning a 'list of names'.)

October Revolution

The Bolshevik revolution in October 1917, which overthrew the Provisional Government an brought the Bolsheviks to power.

OGPU

United State Political Administration: from 1922, the Soviet secret police in succession to the *Cheka*. In 1934 it was taken over by the NKVD.

Okhrana

The tsarist secret police. Agents regularly infiltrated revolutionary groups and spied in meetings.

Old Bolshevik

Term used for those who had been members of the Bolshevik Party before 1917, many of whom had been close associates of Lenin. Old Bolsheviks were prominent among the victims of the Purges.

oligarch

Member of a ruling clique or elite.

Orgburo

Organisational Bureau of the Communist Party of the Soviet Union, an internal party body that allocated party members to particular posts.

perestroika

'Restructuring': the policy adopted by Mikhail Gorbachev in the 1980s of restructuring the Soviet state to render it more efficient and less corrupt. It ended in the collapse of the Soviet Union in 1991.

plenum

A full, or plenary, session.

Politburo

The highest decision- and policy-making body within the CPSU and therefore within the Soviet Union.

Pravda

'Truth': the main newspaper of the Soviet Union. It was controlled by the Communist Party.

Provisional Government

Temporary government set up after the fall of the tsar in February 1917, pending elections to a Constituent Assembly. The Provisional Government had to take over the running of Russia's participation in the First World War. It was overturned by the Bolsheviks in October 1917.

Purges

The wave of arrests and executions, especially of members of the CPSU, that followed the assassination of Sergei Kirov in 1934. The word has connotations of internal cleansing.

rabfak

Workers' Faculty which offered further education courses to Soviet workers.

Red Army

The Soviet army formed during the Civil War.

revisionist

Term used of any historian who challenges accepted orthodoxy. In this context it refers to those who have challenged the totalitarian interpretation of Stalin.

Right Opposition

Term used for those who, like Bukharin, supported the NEP and resisted attempts to drop it and move to a centralised policy of rapid industrialisation.

RSDLP

Russian Social Democratic Labour Party, the formal name of the pre-Revolutionary Russian Communist Party.

Russification

The policy of imposing Russian language and culture on the non-Russian people of the Russian empire and later the Soviet Union.

Ryutin platform

A policy document calling for greater freedom of thought and expression issued in 1932 by Martemyan Ryutin.

Secret Speech

Speech given by Khrushchev in closed session (i.e. without the press present) to the Twentieth Congress of the CPSU in which he denounced Stalin's brutality and cult of personality.

Shakhty Affair

A supposed sabotage plot by foreign experts working at the Shakhty mines in southern Russia in 1928. It led to a purge of foreign experts working within Russian industry.

show trial

A rigged trial held in public and broadcast through the media. The aim is not to ensure justice but to get the widest possible audience for damaging confessions from the defendants.

smychka

The alliance of industrial and agricultural workers symbolised by the Soviet hammer and sickle emblem.

socialisation

In this context, transformation of society and economy along socialist lines.

Socialism in One Country

Stalin's policy of building a socialist society and economy in the Soviet Union rather than working for Communist revolution elsewhere in the world.

Socialist Realism

An officially approved naturalistic artistic style often showing smiling workers and peasants in a sunny scenic setting, much used to promote policies such as industrialisation and collectivisation. It replaced abstract and *avant-garde* styles, which were thought to alienate ordinary citizens.

Socialist Revolutionaries (SRs)

A radical political party and terrorist group which believed in giving power to the peasantry. It was divided between 'Left SRs', who were prepared to cede some ground to the proletariat, and 'Right SRs', who were not. With some exceptions, the SRs were bitter enemies of the Bolsheviks.

soviet

The Russian word for council. This was the term used for the councils of workers and members of the armed forces elected throughout Russia during the 1905 revolution. The Bolsheviks based their bid for power in 1917 on the soviets and adopted the word into their vocabulary so that it became synonymous with 'Communist'.

Sovnarkom

See Council of People's Commissars.

spetsy

Technical specialists.

Stakhanovite

One who emulated the miner Aleksei Stakhanov, whose prodigious feat in supposedly digging a huge amount of coal in a single shift made him a Soviet hero.

stal'

The Russian word for steel.

totalitarian

The political philosophy which believes in handing over full power to a single dictator. It is applied to the school of historical writing which sees Stalin in ultimate control of all developments within the Soviet Union, especially the operation of the Great Terror.

troika

Literally a 'group of three'. Troikas of local officials were widely used to inter-rogate and condemn suspects during the Great Terror.

twenty-five-thousanders

Volunteer party members who went into the countryside to promote the virtues of collectivisation.

United Opposition

An alliance of Zinoviev and Kamenev with their former bitter opponent Trotsky formed in 1926 in a vain attempt to prevent Stalin's rise to power.

Urals-Siberian method

Coercive tactics employed against Siberian peasants during collectivisation and widely copied in other parts of the Soviet Union.

Vesenkha

Supreme Council of the National Economy.

vozhd'

A Russian word akin to the German word Führer, to denote a supreme leader. It was increasingly used of Stalin.

vydvizhentsy

'Upwardly mobile workers', i.e. workers who were promoted into white-collar jobs within the bureaucracy.

war communism

The policy of ruthless food requisitioning and the nationalisation of industry during the Civil War. It provoked the Kronstadt Mutiny.

White Guards

Anti-Bolshevik troops during the Civil War.

Yezhovshchina

The 'time of Yezhov', i.e. the period when the Great Terror was directed by Nikolai Yezhov.

Zhdanovshchina

Period of repression after the end of the Second World War. It was supervised by Andrei Zhdanov.

znat'

The 'ruling class' of high-ranking, privileged members of the CPSU.

People

Alliluyeva, Nadezhda (Nadya) (1901–32)
Stalin's second wife. Her suicide left him devastated and has been identified as one of the causes of the Purges.

Alliluyeva, Svetlana (1926–)
Daughter of Stalin by his second wife, Nadya. After his death she became a well-known figure in the West.

Beria, Lavrenty (1899–1953)
Ruthless and much-feared leader of the NKVD.

Bonaparte, Napoleon (1769–1821)
French emperor who seized power by overthrowing the government of revolutionary France. Fears of 'Bonapartism' contributed to the suspicion in which Trotsky was held by his colleagues.

Brezhnev, Leonid (1906–82)
Leader of the Soviet Union from 1964 to 1982.

Bronstein, Lev Davidovich
Original name of Trotsky.

Budenny, Semyon (1888–1973)
Georgian Bolshevik and close associate of Stalin.

Bukharin, Nikolai (1888–1938)
Leading Bolshevik, supporter of the NEP and member of the Right Opposition. Tried and shot in the third Moscow show trial.

Bulganin, Nikolai (1895–1975)
Prime minister of the Soviet Union from 1955, though he acted essentially as a supporter of Nikita Khrushchev, First Secretary of the Communist Party of the Soviet Union.

Chiang Kai-shek (1887–1975)
Chinese Nationalist leader and fierce enemy of the Chinese Communist Party.

Dan, Fedor (1871–1949)
Founder of the Mensheviks, along with Yuly Martov. He opposed Bolshevik rule and was forced into exile.

Darwin, Charles (1809–82)

Nineteenth-century British scientist, author of *On the Origin of Species* (1859). He was revered in the Soviet Union for having issued a scientific challenge to the basis for religious faith.

Dzhugashvili, Iosif Vissarionovich (1879–1953)

Original name of Josef Stalin.

Dzhugashvili, Vissarion (1853/4–90)

Stalin's father.

Dzhugashvili, Yekaterina (1858–1937)

Stalin's mother.

Eismont, Nikolai (1892–1935)

Member, along with Smirnov and Tolmachev, of an informal group critical of Stalin's method of rule. The group called for an end to collectivisations and the restoration of free trade unions.

Frunze, Mikhail (1885–1925)

Successor to Trotsky as commander of the Red Army.

Gorbachev, Mikhail (1931–)

Reformist General Secretary of the CPSU from 1985. His policies of glasnost and perestroika led to the collapse of the Soviet Union in 1991.

Gorky, Maksim (1868–1936)

Celebrated Russian writer and a close associate of Lenin.

Ivan IV 'the Terrible' (1530–84)

Sixteenth-century tsar who established the autocratic power of the tsars in Russia. He was much admired by Stalin.

Kaganovich, Lazar (1893–1991)

Leading Bolshevik, staunchly loyal to Stalin.

Kalinin, Mikhail (1875–1946)

Leading Bolshevik, opposed to a harsh anti-peasant policy during collectivisation.

Kamenev, Lev (1883–1936)

Leader of the Bolshevik Party in Moscow. Criticised plans for the October Revolution in 1917 and, with Zinoviev, opposed Stalin's rise to power. Tried in the Moscow show trials and shot.

Khrushchev, Nikita (1894–1971)

Leading Communist. After Stalin's death he held power jointly with Malenkov before ousting Malenkov and taking power himself. He started the postwar anti-Stalin reaction with his 1956 Secret Speech to the Twentieth Party Congress.

Kirov, Sergei (1886–1934)

Charismatic Communist Party leader in Leningrad. His assassination in 1934 sparked off the Purges.

Koba

Revolutionary name adopted by the young Stalin and often used by his close friends even after he had taken the name 'Stalin'. The name came from a Georgian nationalist hero.

Kosygin, Aleksei (1904–80)

Leading Soviet politician after the fall of Khrushchev in 1964, but increasingly eclipsed by Brezhnev.

Krupskaya, Nadezhda (1869–1939)

Lenin's wife and a prominent opponent of Stalin.

Kuzakova, Maria

Mother of Stalin's illegitimate son, Konstantin Kuzakov.

Lominadze, Vissarion (1897–1935)

Critic of Stalin and supporter of the Ryutin platform.

Lugovskaya, Nina (1918–93)

Russian teenager caught up in the Purges, whose diaries have been found in the NKVD archives.

Malenkov, Georgy (1902–88)

Briefly prime minister of the Soviet Union after Stalin's death.

Martov, Yuly (1873–1923)

Leader of the Mensheviks within the RSDLP.

Marx, Karl (1818–83)

Nineteenth-century German philosopher and socialist. His ideas formed the basis of twentieth-century communism.

Molotov, Vyacheslav (1890–1986)

Leading Bolshevik. Foreign minister under Stalin.

Nikolaev, Leonid (1904–34)

Assassin of Sergei Kirov.

Ordzhonikidze, Grigory (Sergo) (1886–1937)

Georgian Bolshevik and close friend of Stalin.

Orwell, George (pen name of Eric Blair) (1903–50)

British writer. His disillusion with Soviet socialism is evident in *Nineteen Eighty-Four*, which imagines a future totalitarian state, and *Animal Farm*, a bitter satire on the Russian Revolution.

Peter I 'the Great' (1672–1725)

Eighteenth-century reformist tsar, founder of St Petersburg and responsible for modernising Russian government and administration along Western lines.

Preobrazhensky, Yevgeny (1886–1937)

Leading Bolshevik and member of the Left Opposition.

Radek, Karl (1885–1939)

Leading Old Bolshevik and a member of the Left Opposition. He was tried and imprisoned in the second show trial.

Rykov, Aleksei (1881–1938)

Leading Old Bolshevik and close associate of Lenin. Member of the Right Opposition. Tried and executed in the third Moscow show trial.

Ryutin, Martemyan (1890–1937)

Leading critic of Stalin and author of the Ryutin platform, which called for a less oppressive policy towards the peasantry.

Skryabin, Vyacheslav

Original name of Molotov.

Smirnov, Aleksandr (1878–1938)

Prominent member of the CPSU and critic of Stalin.

Solzhenitsyn, Aleksandr (1918–)

Eminent Russian writer, Nobel Prize winner and dissident, author of *The Gulag Archipelago*, which criticised Stalin's repression.

Soso

Childhood nickname for Stalin.

Stakhanov, Aleksei (1906–77)

Mineworker from southern Russia. He became a national hero in 1935 when it was reported that he had produced in one shift 14 times his quota. His feat was widely reported and formed the basis of the Stakhanovite movement.

Stalin, Vasily (1921–62)

Son of Stalin by his second wife, Nadya. He served as an airforce general in the Second World War and plundered Germany for luxury goods for himself. He spent much of the period after his father's death in jail.

Stalin, Yakov (1907–43)

Son of Stalin and his first wife, Yekaterina Svanidze. Largely abandoned by Stalin after Yekaterina's death from tuberculosis. He was captured by the Germans in the Second World War; he was disowned by his father and died in German custody.

Sukhanov, Nikolai (1882–1940)

Menshevik critic of the Bolsheviks. Arrested in 1937 and shot in 1940.

Svanidze, Yekaterina (no birth date available–1907)

Stalin's first wife and mother of his son, Yakov.

Sverdlov, Yakov (1885–1919)

Leading administrator within the Bolshevik Party in the years after the October Revolution.

Syrtsov, Sergei (1893–1937)

Critic of Stalin and supporter of the Ryutin platform.

Tito, Josip (1892–1980)

Yugoslav Communist leader. His refusal to accept orders from Moscow infuriated Stalin and provided an alternative model for a Communist state.

Tolmachev, Vladimir (1886–1937)

Member of an informal group critical of Stalin. It also included Smirnov and Eismont.

Tomsky, Mikhail (1880–1936)

Trade Union leader and prominent Old Bolshevik. Supporter of the NEP and member of the Right Opposition.

55004

Trotsky, Leon (1879–1940)

Leading Bolshevik, though he had originally been a Menshevik. Right-hand man to Lenin, leader of the Red Army during the Civil War and responsible for crushing the Kronstadt Mutiny. Opposed the NEP and led the Left Opposition to Stalin. Forced into exile and murdered on Stalin's orders in 1940.

Tukhachevsky, Mikhail (1893–1937)

Military hero of the Red Army during the Civil War. Tried and shot during the army purges of the 1930s.

Ul'yanov, Vladimir Il'ich (1870–1924)

Original name of Lenin.

Voroshilov, Kliment (1881–1969)

Georgian Bolshevik and close associate of Stalin.

Vyshinsky, Andrei (1883–1954)

State prosecutor during the Moscow show trials.

Yagoda, Genrikh (1891–1938)

First People's Commissar for Internal Affairs, in charge of the early stages of the Purges. Tried and executed in the third Moscow show trial.

Yezhov, Nikolai (1895–1940)

Leader of the NKVD during the Purges. Later himself purged and shot.

Zhdanov, Andrei (1896–1948)

Close associate of Stalin after the Second World War, in charge of enforcing conformity with party ideology.

Zinoviev, Grigory (1883–1936)

Leading Old Bolshevik and Commissar for Foreign Affairs. Along with Kamenev he questioned the wisdom of the October Revolution and opposed the rise of Stalin and was executed in the show trials.